For King or Country

Major Philip Van Cortlandt

1739-1814

A Memoir

Stephen Le Vine

Front cover image by Jesus Esteban San Jose.

First Published 2025
Published by Loncastle South
Eastbourne, East Sussex. U.K.
e-mail: loncastlesouth@yahoo.co.uk
http://www.stephenlevine.co.uk

British Library Cataloguing in Publication Data. A catalogue record
for this book is available from the British Library.
ISBN: 978-0-9935441-7-0

DEDICATION

Dedicated to the many fallen fighting for their beliefs.

DISCLAIMER

The 13 Colonies

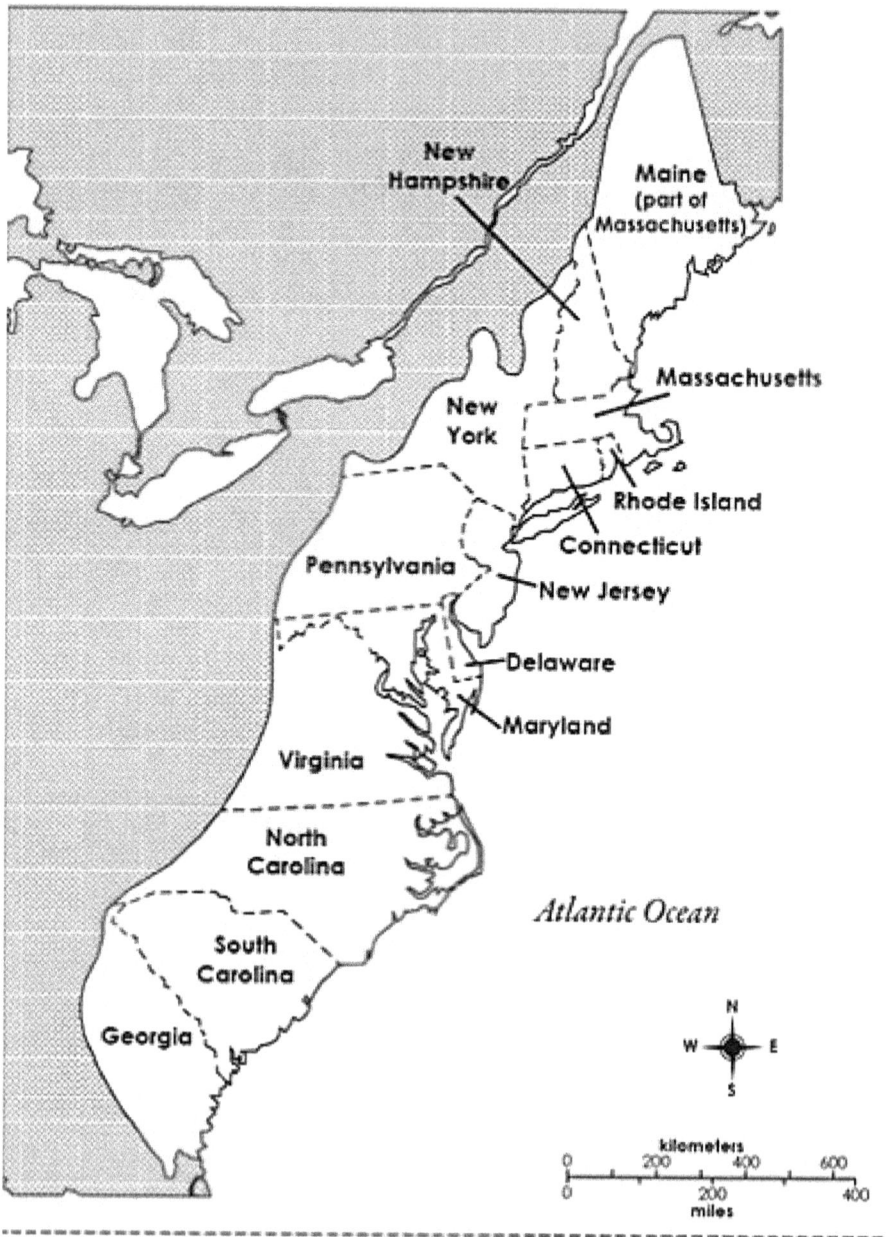

New Hampshire

Maine
(part of Massachusetts)

Massachusetts

New York

Rhode Island

Connecticut

Pennsylvania

New Jersey

Delaware

Maryland

Virginia

North Carolina

Atlantic Ocean

South Carolina

Georgia

N
W — E
S

kilometers
0   200   400   600
0   200   400
miles

CONTENTS

A young Philip Van Cortlandt

Mrs Robert Browne

ACKNOWLEDGMENTS

Many thanks go to the people who have helped me with information and photographs for this publication. Special thanks to the New York Public Library, the New Jersey Historical Society, The National Archives of America, England and India, and the online newspaper archives. Also, to Todd Braisted for his assistance and Simon Williams for his guidance in editing my book.

Author's note: The book uses both dd/mm/yyyy and mm/dd/yyyy date formats. This mixed-use was in use in America and Britain at the time. In the Declaration of Independence, they used the format mm/dd/yyyy, and it was the format that the Americans preferred, as it is still in use today. The English changed their format to the European style in the mid-twentieth century, although private correspondence used dd/mm/yyyy and business used the mm/dd/yyyy format.

Catharine and family   Mr Barrie Clifford

An undated 7ins x 5 ins pastel painting of Catharine and her girls. There is some doubt as to who the children are, but I believe they are, from left to right…Catharine (1764), Margaret Hughes (1768), Gertrude (1772), (Catharine), Elizabeth (1764) and Mary Ricketts (1763).

1 PREFACE

So, who was Philip? He was a devoted and loving husband, father, successful businessman and farmer. Descended from a rich and influential Dutch family, he was a well-educated and principled man. He reluctantly took up arms to support the British Crown. Philip believed in the unity of the Empire and the monarchy rather than republicanism. He supported the constitutional government and was against rebellion. Like many other Americans who fought for the Crown, Philip lost all his property in New Jersey and New York and his entitlement to part of the Manor of Cortlandt. He died thousands of miles from his native America, in England, and was buried alone.

In this book, we are only concerned with the history of Philip van Cortlandt (1739-1814) and his family. He was the cousin of General Philip Van Cortlandt (1749-1831), who served in the Continental Army and later sat in the New York State Senate and the U.S. House of Representatives. The cousin was the eldest son of Pierre Van Cortlandt and a staunch believer in American independence.

To provide context to Philip's changing circumstances, we briefly discuss the causes of the American Revolutionary War.

Why the Americans and the recently arrived immigrants fought for the British Crown, whilst others fought for independence, is a complex issue. It is not the book's focus. You can find many excellent books about the American Revolutionary War at libraries and bookshops.

Anyone who supported the British in any way during the Revolutionary War was branded as a Loyalist.

They could be residents of North America, or people from Newfoundland, or the islands of the West Indies.

The price these Loyalists – also known as 'Tories' — paid for their beliefs was high. Differences split families. Some never reconciled with their loved ones. Americans had to choose between remaining British subjects loyal to the king or becoming defectors to the new American republic. The heartbreaking choice they had was to declare themselves citizens of a new nation and, hence, traitors to the crown. There was no middle ground.

There were cases when families fought brother against brother and father against son.

In the early years of the conflict, it is estimated[1] that approximately 500,000 citizens opposed independence from the Crown. Other groups of people showed little interest in British imperial policies or the idea of American independence. However, they reacted to pressures imposed upon them by the church, landowners, or their families.

Over 1,500 Americans enlisted as officers in either the British army or their supporting American units.

With over 19,000 men serving in 40+ Loyalist units. Cortlandt Skinner formed the largest unit, the New Jersey Volunteers.

Initially, the New Jersey Volunteers battalions would recruit men by geographic area. This was based on the commanding officer's residence. The 1st and 2nd Battalions were from Monmouth, New Jersey, the 3rd Battalion from Essex, Massachusetts, and the 4th Battalion from Bergen & Morris, New Jersey. The 5th Battalion men came from Sussex and the 6th Battalion from Hunterdon, both counties in New Jersey.

The most significant risk to these volunteers was that if the Colonial army captured them, they would be treated as criminals and not prisoners of war.

---

[1] The Loyal Americans, Allen R.

Not everyone wanted to fight in the war alongside their comrades. Some families preferred to avoid conflict with fellow citizens; they simply sought a peaceful life. One way to escape the fighting was to travel to England. Naturally, some of the population aimed to remain neutral during the conflict. The leading group advocating this stance was the Quakers, who opposed war in any form. However, because of personal circumstances, many of their prominent merchants and lawyers became active members of the Tory regiments. Serving with Cortlandt Skinner were notable Quakers such as Edward Tongan, Joseph Barton, and Elisha Lawrence.

The Friends refused to pay taxes that indirectly supported the war effort. Consequently, the authorities fined them and confiscated their property. Another group trying to stay neutral were landowners who did not want to lose their lands.

From 1775 to 1785, an evacuation plan was in place for many American Loyalists and their families to travel safely to other British territories. The first Americans, approximately 1,000 families, who travelled to Nova Scotia in 1776, were from Boston.

After the conflict, Republicans forced many residents who supported the king into exile. Loyalists lost their land and property and could never return to their country of birth. This action forced some 100,000 persons, 2.4% of the population, to settle in foreign lands, such as British North America (now Canada), the West Indies and Great Britain[2].

A background history of the early Dutch settlement.

Dutch merchants sent ships to the newly found lands to trade with the Indians.

The Dutch had been in the area since 1609, when the navigator, Henry Hudson, arrived. As business prospered, the Dutch authorities wished to expand their control.

---

[2] The Loyal Americans, Allen, R.

In 1621, the States-General in the Netherlands formed a new company, the Dutch West India Company, with a new charter. Article II of their licence expressly stipulated that this company should 'promote the settlement of fertile uninhabited districts.'

On 20 June 1623, the ship *'Nieuw Nederlandt'* with Captain Mey and Adriaen Joriszen Tienpont set sail for the new colony.

The newly formed company then established two forts. One was on the east coast of North America, which they named Fort Orange (now Albany). The other was Fort Nassau in the south, in Delaware. Then, in 1625, the settlers established a new settlement at the southern end of Manhattan Island.

These first settlers had departed from the Netherlands on board the ship *'Nieuw Nederlandt'*. It arrived in April. On the boat were thirty Flemish families, who spoke Dutch and lived in the country's northern area, and Walloon families, who spoke French and lived in the southern part of the country.

The ship returned home carrying a cargo of five hundred otter skins, one thousand five hundred beaver skins, and other freight valued at about twelve thousand dollars.

During the rest of 1624 and into 1625, six additional vessels arrived with new immigrants, livestock, and supplies. By 1626, exports from the colonies amounted to $19,000.

In the spring of 1624, Peter Minuit (1560-1638) of Wesel, Westphalia, the third person appointed Director General of the Dutch West India Company, travelled to the new colony.

The settlers established a new township at the southern end of Manhattan Island in 1625. They designated it as the province's capital, naming it Nieuw Amsterdam.

An engineer, Cryn Fredericxsz, had been sent from Holland to assist in building the new settlement.

The fort, a blockhouse surrounded by red cedar palisades, was probably the first building they constructed. A larger building replaced this in 1635.

Records verify that in November 1626, Minuit purchased Manhattan Island from the local Algonquin Indians. He gave the Indians goods like cloth, tools, and trinkets worth 60 guilders. That would be about US$4,000 in today's currency.

Nieuw Netherlands quickly developed into a culturally and politically diverse settlement. This new colony extended from Albany to Delaware, which included parts of present-day New York, New Jersey, and Pennsylvania. As well as Maryland, Connecticut, and Delaware.

The Dutch West India Company controlled the colony. They made the laws and collected the taxes. They also paid and sent over doctors and craftsmen to help populate the province. Also, they provided soldiers to protect the inhabitants.

Life was tough for the new settlers, and many returned to their homes in the Netherlands. By 1630, the total population of Nieuw Netherlands was about 300, with most of them living around the Fort Amsterdam area.

Director-General Minuit left the colonies in March 1632 and returned home. He later returned to Delaware in 1638 and set up a Swedish colony.

In 1633, a short distance from the fort in Nieuw Amsterdam, they built the first church in the town near the shore of the East River. It was a wooden structure and was in use for ten years. The town received a charter of incorporation in 1653. By 1664, the population of Nieuw Netherlands had increased to two and a half thousand residents.

On Monday, 8 September 1664, English forces captured the town, and Nieuw Amsterdam surrendered.

The British renamed the city and the province as New York in honour of James, the Duke of York, who had led the operation.

The terms were favourable to the Dutch, as after swearing an oath to the crown, they could retain their properties. They could also elect local magistrates and continue their own form of worship.

In the autumn of 1664, the Duke of York appointed Colonel Richard Nicolls (1624-1672) as the first English governor of the Province of New York.

Wars in Europe and a flood of immigration contributed to an estimated population of 9,000 in New York. With a significant number of inhabitants being Germans, Swedes, Finns, and, of course, Dutch. Later, the town became the first in the colonies to receive a royal charter. The king granted this in 1686.

After the British won the Seven Years' War (1756-1763) against France, they began imposing higher tariffs on the American colonies. It was to pay off the debts the British army and navy had incurred. The government in London managed its North American colonies poorly. They disregarded the needs of the inhabitants and restricted the goods Americans could make. They imposed heavy taxes on the population, which caused much distress to the inhabitants.

During the American War of Independence (1775-), Philip served on Staten Island. As well as Manhattan Island and New Jersey, where many battles and skirmishes occurred. There are instances where there are no surviving records of the company or participants involved in fighting.

Trying to discover where Major Philip van Cortlandt was engaged in battle has proved difficult. Although records show that he took part in battalion actions at Grand Forage, Paulus Hook, Connecticut farms, Springfield and Ford Griswold. The precise details are challenging to find.

****

2 PHILIP'S FAMILY – THE EARLY DUTCH COLONIAL YEARS

To know Philip, we need to understand his family history. Where he came from, and details about his paternal family. Philip's ancestry traces back to the heart of Europe and a powerful and influential family. Like other Dutch immigrants, they played a significant role in the early days of modern America. His family can trace their roots to the Duchy of Courland in Livonia, which is now part of modern-day Latvia in the Baltic. In 1561, Lithuania took control of the Duchy, which later became part of Poland.

The Dukes had friendly relationships with the Dutch. They attended the Dutch royal court and purchased land in the Netherlands. Later, the family immigrated to Holland after conflict at home, where they lost their estates.

Oloff Stevensen Van Cortlandt (1610-4 April 1684).

The first member of the Van Cortlandt family to arrive in Nieuw Amsterdam (now part of modern-day Manhattan), in Nieuw Netherland, was Oloff Stevensen Van Cortlandt. His parents were Steven Cornelissen Van Cortlandt (1580-1652) and Fijchgen Catharina Oloffs (1566-1652), and he was their eldest son.

Like his parents, Oloff was born in Wijk bij Duurstede near Utrecht in the Netherlands.

He was a soldier and an educated employee of the Dutch West India Company. Oloff had connections to the royal court and the business world.

The office of the Estates-General of Holland arranged for Oloff to accompany General William Kieft (1597-1647), the newly appointed governor.

Oloff would take up the position of secretary to the government in Nieuw Netherland. The authorities sent General Kieft to replace Director Wouter Van Twiller, who had received his appointment in April 1633. People had accused Van Twiller of maladministration of the colony.

General Kieft, a Dutch West India Company director, would greatly influence Oloff's future career.

The new governor and Oloff departed from the island of Texel, in the province of North Holland, in late September 1637.

On 28 March 1638,[3] after their ship wintered in Bermuda, Oloff arrived on board the *De Haering* (*The Herring*) in Rensselaerswyck, Nieuw Amsterdam.

Rensselaerswyck was a small Dutch colonial 'patroonship' or landholding on the Hudson River.

In July 1640, Director Kieft appointed Oloff to a new position as the Commissary of Cargoes. He received a monthly salary of thirty guilders ($12).

Then, in 1643, the Dutch West India Company appointed Oloff as the Treasurer and Keeper of the Company's Public Stores. In this new position, he collected taxes from traders and landowners.

---

[3] Cook 1913:167

Oloff married Annetje Loockermans (17 March 1618-4 May 1684), who was born in Turnout, Antwerp, Belgium. Annetje was the daughter of Jacob Loockermans and Maeyken Nicasius.

The ceremony in the Dutch Church in Nieuw Amsterdam probably occurred in early March, as they read the banns on 26 February 1642.

Annetje has been credited with bringing the Dutch tradition of celebrating Sinter Klaas (Saint Nicholas) and the Christmas Santa Claus to America. The family lived on Brouwer Straat. The first street in Nieuw Amsterdam to be paved. This was in 1658.

The British renamed Brouwer Straat to Stone Street after the capture and renaming of Nieuw Amsterdam in 1664.

In 1645, they appointed Oloff as a member of The Body of Eight Men. An early democratic citizens' council representing the people and advising the colony's director. He became a freeman in 1648. He then resigned from the Dutch West India Company.

Oloff was an elder of the Reformed Dutch Church and an entrepreneur who went into commerce and the beaver fur trade. 1649 saw him selected as a member and then the following year as President of the new Body of Nine Men. This replaced the previous board.

At this time, he became a colonel in the burgher guard. Later, he served as the Burgomaster of Nieuw Amsterdam. A Burgomaster was a chief magistrate or mayor of a town, a post he held several times. The first appointment was on 2 February 1655, and he retained this position until 1657. They reappointed him in February 1658, a job he held until 1661. He opened a beer brewing business in 1656 and prospered.

In February 1662, they again appointed him as Burgomaster. He served until February 1664. One of his other notable achievements was serving as City Treasurer from 1657 to 1659 and again from 1661 to 1661.

After the British capture of Nieuw Amsterdam, they elected him Burgomaster. On 2 February 1665, he swore an oath of allegiance to the king of England. He held this post until a new administration came into office in June.

The British authorities abolished the Dutch system of government. They then established an English-style municipality with a mayor, aldermen, and sheriff. Oloff became an alderman and the acting mayor of New York. Upon his death, it was reported that he was the fourth-wealthiest man in New York, with an estate valued at 45,000 guilders.

Oloff and Annetje had seven children: two sons, Stephanus (1643-1700), and their second son, Jacobus (1658-1739), along with five daughters.

There are books written and records available that tell the story of the Van Cortlandt family, but we are only interested in Philip's direct male line.

Stephanus Van Cortlandt (7 May 1643-25 Nov 1700)

Stephanus was Oloff's eldest son. He was born on Brouwer Street, Nieuw Amsterdam, New Netherlands. He died in November 1700, at the age of 57, in Croton-on-Hudson, Cortlandt, Westchester, New York. Baptised on 10 May 1643 in the Dutch Reformed Church, Nieuw Amsterdam, Stephanus attended the Nieuw Amsterdam School of the Dutch Reformed Church. His father also brought over from Europe a tutor to assist his son's classical training. Stephanus was deeply involved with the church and had a successful and profitable mercantile career guided by his father. In August 1668, he joined the city militia as an ensign under Captain Marten Cregier and was soon promoted to captain. Then, in 1692, Stephanus became a colonel in the Kings County militia. In 1677, at 34, he became the first native-born mayor of New York City and held that position again from 1686 until 1688.

Although Stephanus was not a lawyer, he held many judicial offices.

He was appointed the first Judge of the Court of Admiralty in October 1678 and Judge of the Superior Court of Pleas of Kings County in September 1688.

Stephanus held significant public positions in New York City and the State of New York. He was appointed on 15 May 1691 as the chief justice of the Provincial Supreme Court.

On instructions from the Duke of York and Governor Dongan, they set up a Governor's Council, which Stephanus served on as Secretary of the Province of New York. He remained on the committee until he died in 1700.

Stephanus, in 1683, bought thirty square miles of land along the Hudson River. In the document of sale, the Indians got "Two ankers of rum (about 70 litres), five half fatts of strong beer," also some guns, powder and "a few gaudy clothes and trinkets." In 1933, the land was worth $77,000,000 (£15,400,000).[4]

In June 1697, Stephanus built the Van Cortlandt Manor house in Croton-on-Hudson, in northern Westchester County.

He used it as a country residence for hunting trips, the storage of furs and an Indian trading post. There was also a saw and gristmill on the site.

Although Stephanus had purchased the land from the indigenous Indians, he agreed they could remain living in the area surrounding the new manor house.

The building was not a principal residence for the family until Pierre Van Cortlandt, Stephanus's grandson, moved there in 1749. Pierre enlarged the house to three stories and added two large brick chimneys and a porch.

In 1697, Stephanus received a patent from the king, William III, on 17 June, converting his land into a manor.

---

[4] Cumberland Evening News. 20 Feb 1933.

The land now consisted of 8,000 acres. Within the manor grounds, he divided parts into farms. Tenants held some farms, and Stephanus granted them long leases.

The Charter granted Stephanus the privilege of holding a Court Leet, a manorial court that deals with criminal cases and imposes penalties for minor offences, as well as patronage over all churches within the manor.

Although there are no records stating that Stephanus ever provoked this privilege. Also, written in the Charter, it stated, "It provides in the fullest manner for all hunting and fishing rights."

There was a special privilege granted, giving "The Lords of Cortlandt, the extraordinary privilege of sending a representative to the Provincial Assembly."

Initially, the builders constructed the manor house with Nyack red sandstone, with solid three-foot thick walls and eight rooms. It stood near the mouth of the river Croton, and the building was forty feet long by thirty-three feet wide, with a low-pitched roof and dormer windows.

The house stands on a brow overlooking the broad estuary of the Croton River, with views to the southeast. Looking to broaden his estate, Stephanus bought more lands from the native Indians on the east side of the Hudson and along the Croton River.

His brother Jacobus (1658-1739) was a New York merchant. In 1719, he became mayor of New York City and, in 1747, built Cortlandt House (now a museum) in Yonkers. In 1889, the City of New York purchased the Yonkers estate. Which is now known as Van Cortlandt Park. Jacobus married Eva Philipse and had one son, Frederick.

Stephanus married Gertrude (Geertruy) Schuyler (4 February 1654-August 1723), the daughter of Philip Pieterse Schuyler and Margarita Van Slechtenhorst, in Albany on 10 September 1671. They lived at the 'Waterside', a well-furnished house at the corner of Pearl Street and Broad Street.

Gertrude and Stephanus had fourteen children. Four were boys, but we are only interested in the third son, Philip. His two elder brothers, John and Oliver, died in 1702 and 1708.

Philip Van Cortlandt (9 August 1683-2 Sept 1748)

Philip was born on 9 August and baptised on 22 August 1683 in the Dutch Church in New York City.

He was the second lord of the manor, owning farms and South Lot Number 1, where the manor house stood, and, like his father, he was a successful merchant and politician.

Van Cortlandt Manor

Philip became an Alderman (a member of the municipal assembly or council) in 1717, serving until 1729. On 26 June 1729, the governor appointed him to the Provincial Council, which he served on until 1746.

Later, after the treaty with the Iroquois Indians, he took up the position of Commissioner of Indian Affairs. There are rumours suggesting he held a commission as a colonel in the New York militia.

Philip spent most of his time living in New York and used the manor house as a summer retreat.

He was a fur trader and also owned The Coffee House, some farms, and other buildings. He was also the proprietor of the tavern, The Fighting Cocks.

In September 1776, rumours soon spread, stating that the Great New York City Fire started at the wooden Fighting Cocks tavern near White Hall slip.

It was just six days after the British invasion of New York. British authorities blamed the rebels for the fire. The blaze destroyed about 500 homes and about a quarter of Manhattan.

Philip married Catharine de Peyster (7 September 1688–11 April 1734), the daughter of Colonel Abraham de Peyster and Catharina de Peyster, on 7 December 1710, in the Dutch Church in New York.

They had six children, of whom five were sons. Stephen (Stephenus) (1711-1756), Abraham (1713-1746), Philip (Philippus) (1716-1745), John (Johannes 1718-1747), and Pierre (1721-). Their daughter Catharine, born 26 June 1725, died aged nine in an accident in 1735.

On Philip's death, he divided his estate between his surviving sons in his will, dated 1 August 1746, and probated on 17 November 1748.

Stephen inherited the house in New York, which was leased out at the time. Pierre inherited the manor house in Croton, various farms, and the South Lot Number 1.

Stephen Van Cortlandt (26 October 1711-17 October 1756)

Philip and Catharine's eldest son, Stephen, our Philip's father, succeeded his father and became head of the family.

Stephen was born in New York and, like his father, was baptised in the Reformed Dutch Church in New York City on 24 October 1711.

He was a quiet and studious man who did not participate in civil or military affairs. Stephen lived in a house on the north side of Stone Street, New York City, with his wife, Mary Walton Ricketts.

This was a different property from the house he inherited from his father. Stephen had strong Royalist inclinations, which he passed on to his children.

Stephen had inherited three farms, each 250 acres, in South Lot No.1 and the Cortlandt Manor house in New York City, which another family was leasing at the time.

When our Philip's grandfather died, he left much of his estate and the Cortlandt Manor to Stephen's younger brother, Pierre. It meant that our Philip, who would have been the eldest male relative, was in line to inherit the estate, but for the circumstances of the American War of Independence.

The Reverend William Vesey conducted Stephen's marriage ceremony. This was to Mary Walton Ricketts (1713-1789), the daughter of William Ricketts (1678-1735) and Mary Ann Walton (1675-1742). The ceremony probably took place on May 6, 1738. This was the date the authorities granted a New York licence.

They had two children. The boys were Philip, born on 10 November 1739, and William Ricketts (12 March 1742–1830). William married Elizabeth Kortright on 3 January 1765, and they had three children. We detail Philip's life later.

On Stephen's death, his will, dated 7 June 1754 and proved on 24 May 1757, states he leaves, "all my farmland and plantation in the Manor of Cortlandt now in tenure of Jacob Cornwell to my son Philip."

This included three farms, each of 250 acres, in the South Lot No. 1 on the Cortlandt Manor Estate. Jacob Cornwell leased the farms. Stephen bequeathed his property in New York to both of his sons, Philip and William Ricketts.

After Stephen's death, Mary remarried on 13 September 1757 to the Reverend Philip Hughes.[5]

The Van Cortlandt family was wealthy and influential in the city and in the state of New York. Over the years, successful marriages with other prominent Dutch-American families in the area helped develop New York and the surrounding districts.

Because of poor governance by Great Britain and costly trade restrictions, together with high taxes, this later caused rifts and disagreements. The people in the colony became discontented. How could they resolve these issues? This burning question divided families, with some supporting the king and others backing the American revolutionary cause.

There are reports that Governor Tryon (1729-1788), governor of New York, visited Croton and the Van Cortlandts in 1774.

He reportedly suggested that if they supported the King's cause, he would reward them with land and possibly a title. As Pierre and his son Philip had been chosen to represent the county's residents at the Colonial Assembly, they refused the idea. A position that they were determined to pursue.

It is ironic that Pierre and his brother Stephen both had sons called Philip. The two sons served in the military. But they had very different ideas about the future of their country. One rose to the rank of Brigadier-General in the Republican army.

---

[5] "New Jersey, U.S., Episcopal Diocese of New Jersey, Church Records, 1700-1970"

This Philip (1749-1831) later received an appointment to an influential position in his government.

Later, they elected him as a member of the House of Representatives. The other, the subject of this book, was a forgotten man with drastically reduced estates who lived and eventually died in a foreign land.

There was also another Colonel Philip Van Cortlandt (1725-1800), who came from a different branch of the family, the New Jersey branch.

This Philip's ancestry can be traced back to Stephen, the fourth son of Stephanus, who was born on 11 August 1685 and died in 1766.

His home was in Second River (now Belleville) in Essex County, and he fought on the Republican side as commanding officer of the Second Essex County Militia Regiment. He also served in Nathaniel Heard's Brigade. Philip was recorded as the highest-ranking Revolutionary War officer from Essex County. After he died on November 20, 1800, they buried him in the Van Cortlandt crypt at the Belleville Dutch Reform Church cemetery.

Members of prominent families, including the Van Cortlandts, were involved in both sides of the war. With uncles and cousins often fighting against each other. Our Philip's cousin of the same name from the Cortlandt Manor fought on the side of American independence, and another cousin supported the Loyalist cause.

After the conflict, there was no reconciliation between these two branches of the family. In later years, when Philip was living in England, he tried to reconcile with his cousin, Pierre's son, but to no avail. Philip never received a reply to his letters.

Our Philip and most of his descendants stayed in England. Finding employment was very difficult for the newly arrived American Loyalists, but eventually Philip found employment with the Barrack Master General's Office. His friend Oliver De Lancey helped him secure this position.

Established in 1793, the office managed barracks in Great Britain. The authorities stationed Philip in Sussex, in the south of England.

In the years that followed, one of Philip's sons and his grandson served with the British Army, fighting in India. Another son, also a soldier in the British Army, died in Spain.

During the years of conflict, over ten prominent families in the area became divided.

When the war ended, a few Loyalist families returned to North America to face the wrath of their fellow countrymen. However, many settled in foreign lands. Most chose to settle in Quebec and Nova Scotia.

After gaining independence, life settled down until June 1812. When another conflict broke out, it was between America, her allies, and Great Britain and her allies over alleged British violations of U.S. maritime rights.

Then, in the mid-nineteenth century, the most terrible event any country could experience occurred: the four-year Civil War of 12 April 1861-9 April 1865. With fighting between the northern and western states on the one hand and the 11 southern states on the other. These southern states had seceded and formed the Confederate States of America. Over 600,000 soldiers died, and the fighting injured many more.

****

3 EARLY YEARS

It is the 10th of November 1739, and Philip, the first of two sons of Stephen Van Cortlandt, was born in Lower Yonkers, New York City. Stephen and the family were living in a fine brick-built house on the north side of Stone Street.

Our Philip is a descendant of the wealthy and important Van Cortlandt family. Since Oloff arrived in 1638, the Van Cortlandt family had become prosperous and influential residents in the new and bustling New York State. Members of his family held many prominent positions in the area's government. And, with commercial success, they became large landowners.

Unlike his brother Pierre, who inherited the Cortlandt Manor estate, Stephen, Philip's father, chose not to participate in politics or business. Pierre, a colonel, then a general in Westchester's patriot militia, later became the first Lieutenant Governor of New York in 1777.

Except for the circumstances that followed in the years to come, Philip would have become the fourth Lord of the Manor if they had carried forward the title. Philip was the fifth generation of the Van Cortlandt family in America.

Philip and his brother grew up in a devout, God-fearing family. They regularly attended church. Raised by a strong royalist, his father also ensured his children held solid Anglican beliefs. The Rev. William Vesey baptised Philip in the Dutch Reformed Church, New Amsterdam, founded in 1628.

Because of his upbringing, Philip's strong Loyalist ideals would shape and change his life and his family's status.

Our Philip was a conscientious and studious child. After his primary education, in 1754, he attended the newly created King's College in New York. The college, initially housed in Trinity Church, was on Manhattan Island in New York City. Philip was one of the first group of eight students to attend.

Among his fellow students[6], Samuel Provoost (1742-1815), one of the youngest in his class, achieved honours in his exams and graduated at its head. Samuel was born in New York on 26 February 1742 and was the eldest son of John and Eve Rutgers Provoost. He was a strong supporter of American independence. In February 1777, he was appointed chaplain for the New York Committee of Safety.

Later, in 1786, he became the first Protestant Episcopal bishop of New York. He died suddenly on September 6, 1815, in New York City at the age of seventy-three.

Another student who attended the college at the same time was Samuel Verplanck (1739-1820), who went on to become a successful banker and businessman. He was born in New York City on September 19, 1739. After graduating, he travelled to his maternal uncle's house in Amsterdam, Holland, to learn about the banking business. On April 26, 1761, he married his cousin, Judith Crommelin (1739-1803). Samuel returned to New York in 1763 and moved into a sizeable yellow-brick mansion at 3 Wall Street.

He set himself up as a wholesale importer and continued his career in banking. Samuel was one of the twenty-four founders of the New York Chamber of Commerce in 1768.

Samuel played no part and remained neutral in the Revolutionary War, although he was a supporter of the republican cause.

---

[6] Moore's Hist. Sketch Columbia College. p.20

Still, he allowed his house on his country estate in Fishkill, Dutchess County, to be used as the headquarters for the American army. Samuel died on January 27, 1820, at the age of eighty-one. They buried him in the burying ground of the Episcopal Church in Fishkill.

Josiah Ogden, Henry Cruger Jnr, and Joshua Bloomer were also attending the college at the same time. Joshua became a merchant in New York City. A man of religion, in 1769, the bishop of London ordained him. He returned to America in 1769 and became rector of the church in Jamaica. Joshua died on June 23, 1790, at the age of 55, in Westchester, New York.

Student Henry Cruger Jnr (1739-1827) did not graduate from college. In 1757, when he was eighteen, Henry Cruger Jnr moved to Bristol, England, to continue his education and later establish himself as a merchant. In 1765, Henry married Ellen Peach, a wealthy Bristol merchant's daughter.

With the new family connections, he became active in local politics and, in 1768, joined the Society of Merchant Venturers. Henry became a town councillor and later, in 1766, was appointed Sheriff. In 1781, he became mayor of the city.

In October 1774, after an election, Henry won a parliamentary seat as the Radical candidate representing Bristol. He served in the English parliament from 1774 to 1780 and again from 1784 to 1790. Henry supported the independence ideas of the colonialists and, in the English parliament, said, "American war ... should be put an end to at all events; in order to do this, the independency must be allowed, and the thirteen provinces treated as free states."[7] In April 1789, he returned to New York and joined the Federalist Party, one of the two main early American political parties which advocated for a strong federal government.

Later, Henry won an election in 1792 to become a New York State Senate member.

---

[7] Ibid. xvii. 658-9.

A position he held until 1796. He died in New York on April 24, 1827. This makes him the only member of the English Parliament to have also served as a state senator in the American government.

While attending King's College, Philip volunteered in August 1757 for a short-lived expedition up the Hudson.

It was for the relief of the siege by the French General Louis-Joseph de Montcalm on Fort William Henry. The fort was situated on the southern end of Lake George by the frontier between the British Province of New York and the French Province of Canada.

On August 13th, Philip and six hundred men, mostly volunteers and part of the Westchester detachment, marched to City Hall[8]. They boarded a vessel on the Hudson River and started their journey to Fort William Henry, but by the 16th, they received orders to return; later, they were discharged.

Philip had received a commission from Governor James DeLancey (1703-1760), but had not taken part in any action.

In June 1758, Philip attained his Bachelor of Arts degree and was one of seven students to graduate.

To improve his French language skills, Philip that summer moved into the household of Monsieur de Blez and his family in New Rochelle. Where he spent several enjoyable months with the family. His memoir later stated that he was happy with the "beautiful situation of this place" and the "conversation of several agreeable young ladies."

At the request of the president of King's College, Dr Johnson, Philip returned to study in 1761 and got his Master of Arts degree.

Because of his age and failing health, Dr Johnson resigned from the college in 1763, and Reverend Myles Cooper (1735-1785), a twenty-six-year-old classical scholar, replaced him.

---

[8] Letter from the Council at New York to Lt. Gov James DeLancey at Albany 14 Aug 1757. NYHS vol 24.p.512

Other classmates of the year 1758, who graduated with Philip and were admitted to the bar, were the brothers Isaac and Josiah Ogden, Joseph Reade and Rudolphus Ritzema.

Rudolphus (1739-1803) was born in Friesland, Netherlands, and the family moved to New York in 1744. After graduating, he travelled to the Netherlands and enlisted in the Prussian army.

He returned to New York and studied and practised law. Before the Revolutionary War, Rudolphus kept a military school in Tarrytown, Westchester County.

In June 1775, Rudolphus was appointed lieutenant-colonel of the 1st New York Regiment. On November 28, 1775, he became an American colonel in the Third New York Regiment but later resigned his commission. Our Philip's cousin, the other Philip van Cortlandt, the son of Pierre Van Cortlandt, succeeded Rudolphus as the new colonel of the regiment.

Rudolphus' loyalties changed, and in May 1778, he joined the British, who made him a lieutenant-colonel.

After the hostilities ceased, he and his family evacuated to the city of York, England. He married in July 1787 and settled in the county of Devon. Rudolphus died in May 1803 in the small waterside village of Starcross, which is on the west shore of the Exe Estuary in Teignbridge, Devon, England.

A close friend of Philip's was Isaac Wilkins (1743-1830), who achieved his A.B. degree in 1760. In 1762, Isaac married Isabella Morris, the sister of Lewis Morris, a staunch colonialist who later was one of the signers of the Declaration of Independence. Isaac got his Master's degree in 1763.

Isaac became a member of the General Assembly of New York until 1775, when he was forced to flee to England after writing some pro-British political pamphlets. In 1783, he moved to Shelburne, Nova Scotia.

He became a judge in the Supreme Court of Canada. Isaac represented Shelburne Township in the Nova Scotia House of Assembly from 1785 to 1793 before returning to New York and being ordained in the church. Isaac was rector of St. Peter's Church in Westchester Village of the Bronx in New York from 1799 until he died on 5 February 1830.

One weekend, Philip, with his friend Isaac Wilkins and two other comrades, went on a fishing and shooting expedition on the Long Island Sound. The weather was windy, which made taking a boat out very precarious. So, after walking for a while, they came across a field full of sheep.

Well, they had their muskets with them and shot one of the sheep, which they took back to college. There, they prepared a mighty feast for supper. On their return to college, they informed the sheep's owners, the DeLancey family, of their exploits. It was all taken in good humour, and they did not have to pay for their afternoon adventure.

The setting up of a college in New York came about when Governor Lewis Morris (1671-1746) of New Jersey made inquiries in England. He wrote in 1702 to the Society for the Propagation of the Gospel in Foreign Parts that:

"New York is the center of English America and a proper place for a college."

Some years later, in 1746, after the General Assembly passed an Act, they set up a public lottery to raise funds for the new college. They raised £3,443 18s, which they handed to the trustees for the set-up of the college. In the New York Gazette of May 31, 1754, Dr Samuel Johnson placed an advert:

"To such Parents as have now (or expect to have), Children prepared to be educated in the College of New York."

"Ornaments to their Country and useful to the public Weal in their Generations" and "to lead them from the study of nature to knowledge of themselves, and of the God of nature and their duty to him, themselves, and one another, and everything that can contribute to their true happiness, both here and hereafter."[9]

In the advert, he advised when the courses would start and where the studies would take place. He also informed new students of the minimum academic requirements they needed, along with an outline of the education they would receive.

The new college, the students were told, would teach arithmetic, Latin and Greek grammar, and studies of the Gospel of St. John. They would also teach languages and the arts of reasoning. Geography and history were other subjects in the curriculum.

After it received a royal charter from King George II and after many years of discussion, they incorporated the college, an Anglican institution, in October 1754:

"for the Instruction and Education of Youth in the Learned Languages and the Liberal Arts and Sciences."

The Trinity Church used part of the land (about one-tenth) on the King's Farm, granted to them in 1755, for the new King's College. Initially, they held classes at the Trinity Church schoolhouse.

On August 23, 1756, they laid the cornerstone of the college's first building. The site chosen was on the corner of Park Place and Church Street. A report later appeared in the New York Gazette.

---

[9] Schneider, Volume IV, pp. 222-224.

"Laft Monday, was laid by his Excellency, Sir Charles Hardy,
our Governor, the Firft Stone of King's College in this City.
On which Occafion the Honourable James De
Lancey 'Efquire; our Lieutenant Governor,
with the Governors of the College and Mr. Cutting the Tutor with
the students met at Mr. Willett's, and thence proceeded to
the House of Mr. Vandenbergh,
at the Common, whither his Excellency came in his Chariot, and
proceeded with them about One O'Clock to the College ground,
near the river on the Northwest Side of the City,
where a Stone was prepared…"

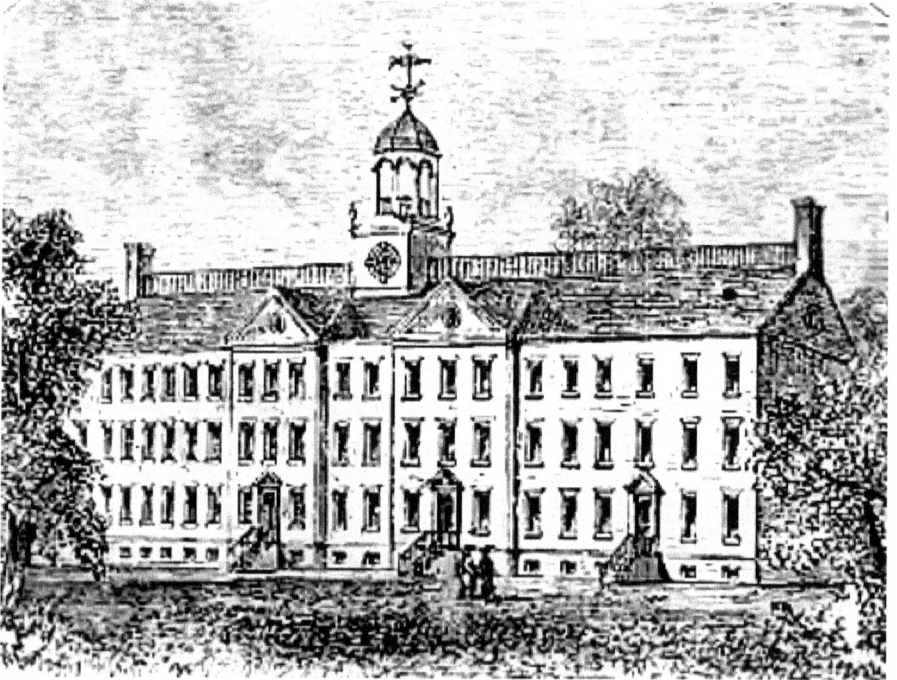

King's College

The British Crown officials in its governing body strongly influenced
the college's governance, so it is not surprising that Philip chose the path
to defend the Crown in later years.

These Government officials appointed the highly respected Reverend Dr Samuel Johnson (1696-1772) as the college's first president.

He was 58 and an Anglican minister and colonial scholar from Stratford, Connecticut. This new position came with a yearly salary of two hundred and fifty pounds.

Dr Johnson had been educated at Collegiate School, founded in 1701, at Old Saybrook, Connecticut. In 1718, they renamed the school Yale College, which is now situated in New Haven.

At this time, New York's population did not exceed twenty thousand souls but was expanding fast.

The college promised to uphold the principles of religious liberty. They had a curriculum of thirteen subjects. This new college had higher subscriptions than Harvard or Princeton, charging students 25 shillings per quarter. For tuition, they charged additional fees of four pounds per year.

They held the first classes on July 1st, in the vestry room at the Trinity Church schoolhouse, founded in 1709, on Broadway and Wall Street. Later, in 1760, they moved to a large field some one hundred and fifty yards from the Hudson River in Lower Manhattan.

At this time, the college could house, sleep and feed thirty students. The college remained at this location until relocating to Madison Avenue and 49th Street in 1857.

During the War of Independence, they suspended teaching at the college at the request of the Committee of Safety. They removed all books and apparatus to City Hall for safekeeping. It was for eight years, from April 6, 1776, until May 15, 1784.

The school buildings were then put to use as a military hospital, firstly by the Continental Army and later by the British during their occupation of Manhattan.

After the state government passed a new Act in 1784, the college reopened with a new charter. They renamed it as Columbia. In 1896, after its move from Madison Avenue to Morningside Heights at 116th Street and Broadway, they renamed it as Columbia University. It is now one of America's leading universities.

The college is the oldest institution of higher education in the State of New York and the fifth-oldest institution for higher learning in the United States.

Grace Church in the Jamaica neighbourhood, the seat of Queens County, New York City, was founded in 1702. It was built on instructions from the Society for the Propagation of the Gospel in Foreign Parts on about half an acre of land deeded to the rector, Thomas Colgan.

The church opened for worship on Friday, April 5th, 1734, and now it needed refurbishment. Philip was able to help.

Grace Church and burial grounds considerably influenced Philip's life, and it became the resting place of some of his and Catharine's children.

An appeal went out to the congregation in April 1761 for help in the building's renovation. They needed to work on the steeple, windows, and the enclosure of the churchyard.

Dr Jacob Ogden (1721-1780), a well-respected physician in Jamaica, New York, and his family were church members. As Philip was courting the doctor's eldest daughter, Catharine, he agreed to assist.

Records show that in 1761, Jacob contributed £2. 10s and Philip £1. 10s towards the repairs. The total raised for renovations was just over £93. 18s.

GRACE CHURCH, JAMAICA.
OPENED FOR DIVINE WORSHIP FRIDAY APRIL 5TH 1734.

After securing a licence on July 30th, in New York, Philip married[10] the fifteen-year-old daughter of Dr Jacob Ogden and Elizabeth Bradford (1722-1809).

The ceremony occurred with Catharine (29 November 1746–22 February 1828) on August 4, 1762, in Long Island, New York.

Noted in Philip's diary in August:

"After two years constant visits to Jamaica on Nassau
Island (near New York), was married to Miss
Catharine Ogden, daughter of Doctor Jacob Ogden."

---

[10] Original data: State of New York. Names of Persons for whom Marriage Licenses were Issued by the Secretary of the Province of New York, Previous to 1784.

Recorded in the family bible and supported by a letter[11] signed by Catharine, she states that the Reverend John Miller of the Anglican Trinity Church, the first Anglican Church on the island of Manhattan, performed the ceremony. However, the rector at the church at this time was Reverend Henry Barclay. Previously, the Reverend Miller had baptised Catharine. This was on November 25, 1746.

Philip and his new wife moved into a home in New York. Although Philip was a wealthy landowner and heir to extensive Westchester and New York City properties, he engaged in mercantile practices.

The following year, Philip records that with three others, they "built a beautiful vessel for the West India trade." Now a shipowner, businessman, and later a landowner, he firmly believed in right and wrong.

His shipping interests were mainly in trading with the West Indies. The trade to the West Indies was prolific, with flour, wheat, timber, horses, and sheep as the principal items exported. In return, the ships brought back rum, sugar, and molasses. He was helping to satisfy the strong demand for imported goods from the city's growing population.

At sixteen, Catharine gave birth to their first child, Mary Ricketts (1763–1807), in Jamaica, Queens County, New York.

Philip's business interests were proving profitable. In the following year of 1764, the family moved to a farm Philip purchased at Beaver Pond, Jamaica, on Long Island. Where he built a large house and barn.

It was an eventful year with the move to Long Island and with Catharine giving birth to twin girls, Elizabeth (1764–1816) and Catherine (1764–1819).

---

[11] TNA, WO42/63/264.

Philip's three eldest children were all christened by Rev. Myles Cooper (1735-1785), the second principal of King's College.

Following the resignation of Rev. Dr Samuel Johnson in February 1763, King's College in May appointed Rev. Cooper principal, a post he held until 1775.

Since the early days, Rev. Cooper had been a staunch Tory supporter and had made many enemies. After being confronted by an angry mob in May 1775 and rescued by Nicholas Ogden, he escaped. He boarded a British Naval ship anchored in New York harbour. Later in the month, he fled to England.

In 1764, Philip sold his interest in his part ownership of the schooner after a dispute with the boat's captain. He was upset with the captain's behaviour, and the reason he gave was regarding "a contraband trade, contrary to our first arrangement."

The following year, Philip bought a tract of woodland in Jamaica South while continuing to expand his farm.

Cadwallader Colden (1688-1776), a staunch royalist and acting governor of the Province of New York in 1766, offered Philip a captaincy in the Light Dragoons, which he accepted and then joined them in their military exercises.

Catharine gave birth to their first son, Philip Jnr. (1766–1833), in July. He was a twin of Stephen, who unfortunately died in 1767. He was not the only child they lost at an early age.

Later, as a young teenager, Philip Jnr, on July 31, 1779[12], joined his father in the military as an ensign. He served first in the 3rd and then the 4th Battalion of the New Jersey Volunteers.

It would be usual practice for young men, generally around the age of fourteen, who wanted to become officers to join the army as ensigns.

---

[12] North American Army List, published in New York by James Rivington, 1783.

They would serve an apprenticeship for 2–3 years before being promoted to lieutenant. The ensigns were to be treated as officers by the other ranks and given the same respect, even though they had not yet received a commission from the King.

Philip's memoir of 1767 notes that he had finished all the building works, but he was still improving his farm.

Catharine and Philip's fourth daughter, Margaret-Hughes (1768–1828), was born in Long Island.

Having finished building his farm, Philip gave up his interest in shipping and other businesses. He became a 'country squire' and semi-retired to Jamaica, Long Island, New York.

In October 1768, Philip travelled to Philadelphia with some friends, which he later recorded in his diary as an enjoyable venture south.

Philip joined the Queens County, New York legislature, as a magistrate in 1769. Sir Henry Moore of the Commission of the Peace for Queens County had appointed him. It enabled Philip to travel extensively with some friends to Annapolis, Chester, Philadelphia, and New Jersey during this time. Philip was so impressed with life in New Jersey that he vowed to move his family there one day.

Their seventh child, Sarah Ogden, was born in March 1771 on Long Island. Sarah died a month later, on 18 April, and the family buried her at Grace Church, Jamaica, Queens County.

Many of the residents of Queens County were staunch supporters of the American Revolution. Because of this and Philip's Loyalist convictions, he decided to move his family.

New Jersey would be their new home. The move to New Jersey pleased him, but he would later regret his decision. Unknown to him, the county was strongly unwavering revolutionary-minded. Philip and the family were destined to return to Jamaica. Matters were coming to a head, and trouble was brewing, but Philip continued his suburban life.

The introduction of the Stamp Act in 1765 by the British government caused immense conflict and distress in the colonies. It stated that all deeds, bonds, mortgages, notes, and university degrees would become invalid unless written on stamped paper and a duty paid to the crown, as was the practice in Britain.

The British government repealed the Stamp Act in March 1766, but replaced it with the Townshend Acts, also known as the Indemnity Acts.

These new Acts taxed goods such as tea, glass, paper and paint imported to the American colonies, put restrictions on the New York Assembly, and, of course, were a way to raise taxes.

Strong resentment was building in Great Britain's thirteen North American colonies.

Philip requested a survey of four lots near Stone Street in the South Ward of the City of New York in December 1771.

STEPHEN LE VINE

Philip owned Lot 1, bounded on two sides by the Henry Ludlow and
Colonel O Delancey properties.

Lot 2, also Philip's lot, faced Petticoat Lane. Both properties were
25½ feet wide and 100 feet (ca. 30 m) long.[13] In 1772, Philip mortgaged
one of his New York houses to Mr Dennis Carlton.

The family moved to New Jersey, where Philip purchased a three-
hundred-acre farm. That was set on a hill in Whippany with a river and
a mill nearby.

To accommodate his large family, he built a new house, which, later
in his claim for compensation, he valued at £434. The land is now part
of the township of Hanover, Morris County, New Jersey.

The town was initially called 'Whippanong' by its first inhabitants.
Native Americans named it the "place of the willows", or sometimes
known as the "place where the arrow wood grows". The name came from
the abundance of trees growing along the riverbank.

According to reports, the first European settlers arrived from
Elizabeth Town and Newark in 1685.

Historical records show they built the first iron ore forge alongside
the Whippanong River in 1710, and they carried the ore down to the
forge from the Suckasunna mine by horseback.

In 1718, the new settlers erected the Presbyterian Church after
receiving a gift of three and a half acres of land by the Whippanong
River. The benefactor was a respected local schoolteacher, John
Richards.

He donated the land for "a meeting house, schoolhouse, burying yard,
training field, and for public use." Unfortunately, he was the first to be
buried here as he died on December 11, 1718.

---

[13] Manuscripts and Archives Division, The New York Public
Library. "Stone Street" *The New York Public Library
Digital Collections*. 1771.
https://digitalcollections.nypl.org/items/62d40f90-7571-
0135-3a5c-0d443fd6d228

34

May 17, 1694, saw the formation of Burlington County. In 1700, they established Whippanong as the "Whippenny Township" with an area of 500 square miles[14]. There was another change in 1714 when authorities divided Burlington County. The township came under the new Hunterdon County authority. By 1720, this changed again, and they renamed Whippenny Township to 'Hanover Township'. There was much changing of county names and their areas of influence. The name Whippenny disappeared, and Whippany, the new name, was adopted locally.

The town then became a district of the Hanover township. They formed the first militia in Morris County in Whippany in 1775, with Captain Morris in command.

Hanover was a growing township with numerous farms and mills. Their principal crops included wheat, corn, rye, and barley, and there were herds of cows, sheep, and horses. The area also featured sawmills and fruit orchards. Its closeness to New York City and other major towns provided farmers with a ready market for their produce.

Another reason for Philip and his family to move to Whippany could be that Catharine's cousins, Abraham and Samuel Ogden, had businesses in the immediate area.

In April 1736, a Dutch Reformed church was built along the east bank of the Pequannock River on Pompton Plains.

Philip and the family lived in a mansion on top of a hill with spacious gardens and a nearby river and mill. The estate became known as Dashwood. Philip wrote in his memoir:

> " being represented to us as the Eden of our
> northern world, the mountains filled with riches and
> the valley producing en'ry luxury of life spontaneously."

---

[14] Proceedings N. J. Hist. Soc., 2d series, vol.2, p. 18

Philip and Catharine had another daughter, Gertrude (1772–1849), who was born in their new home.

In 1773, Governor William Franklin (1731-1813), the last colonial governor of New Jersey and son of Benjamin Franklin, offered Philip a commission to command a Grenadier Militia company, which he accepted.

Philip now purchased a meadow adjoining his farm. Here, they bred mares, sheep, and pigs and had extensive livestock holdings. His new life was prospering, and his family was increasing. In his memoir of April 1773, Philip wrote:

> "1773 April. Become a member of the church and
> King Club at New York composed of none but staunch
> loyalists determined with life and fortune to support
> their lawful king and the British Constitution against
> the machinations of the Jacobins in America."

In 1774, Philip saw the birth of his ninth child in Hanover, a daughter also called Sarah Ogden (1774–1857), his only daughter who did not marry and subsequently died in the town of Torquay, England[15].

Philip then built a granary on the farm and had a nursery built for their expanding family.

They employed a staff of servants to cook and clean the house. The children had their own nursery, and there was a room large enough to host dances and entertain guests.

The family lived in 'considerable style.' Life was good for the growing family, and Philip was successful.

He was employing about "50 poor people continually ditching, wood cutting, spinning, etc., etc., which affords great satisfaction."

---

[15] Principal Probate Registry. Calendar of the Grants of Probate and Letters of Administration made in the Probate Registries of the High Court of Justice in England. London, England.

But times were changing, and much sorrow and conflict were to come. As he later recorded in his memoir:

"reduced in the space of three months from affuence
to the want of the common necessaries of life."

Philip and Catharine had twenty-three children.[16] But we only know the details of seventeen of them. Twelve of their children reached maturity, with Catharine suffering many miscarriages. With these many children, they affectionately called their children their flock.

Philip lovingly called Catherine, Kitty, and she referred to him as Philly, as can be seen in her letters.

They had a long and endearing relationship with many mishaps along the way. Their sons all joined the British army.

Although the male line from Philip is now extinct, most of his daughters married well into the British aristocracy, and the Cortlandt name continues.

For many years, the confidence of the American people was growing. As was dissatisfaction with the decisions and taxes made by a government that was three thousand miles away in London. Matters were now coming to a head.

It had been nearly a year since the protests by Samuel Adams and the Sons of Liberty of Boston.

On June 27th, there was a meeting in Morristown of "a respectable body of freeholders and inhabitants."

They gathered to elect delegates to attend the forthcoming First Continental Congress. Philip participated in this meeting and was on the committee.

---

[16] TNA, WO42/63/263

Fifty-six delegates attended the First Continental Congress meeting held in Carpenters' Hall, Philadelphia, on September 5, 1774. Delegates from twelve of the colonies attended. They elected Peyton Randolph, from Virginia, as President. Georgia was the only colony that did not take part in the gathering.

At the meeting, moderate Tories like Philip opposed the proposal to boycott British goods or to take up arms against the Crown. Along with others who shared similar views, Philip hoped that the conference would find a way to resolve the differences with the Crown. Unfortunately, that was not the case.

There was significant discontent, and on October 20th, Congress approved plans to establish the Continental Association and endorsed the Suffolk Resolves. This marked the beginning of the road to independence.

The Suffolk Resolves, made on September 9, 1774, were a declaration put forth by leaders from Suffolk County, Massachusetts.

In their statement, they declared they would boycott goods imported from Great Britain until the Coercive Acts, introduced in the British Parliament by Lord North, were repealed.

This Act, also known as the Intolerable Acts, was passed in early 1774 and set out the following:

The Boston Port Act closed the Boston Harbour until the people of Boston paid for the tea that they threw into the harbour. It went into effect on June 1, 1774.

The Quartering Act: established on March 24th. It required colonial authorities to provide public housing for British troops to be paid by Provincial funds.

The Administration Act: Superseded colonial law by giving British troops protection from any civil actions.

The Massachusetts Government Act: Restricted town meetings for one a year unless the governor gave approval. The Massachusetts General

Assembly could not meet. The Royal governor would appoint all the officials which included Judges and Sheriffs.

The Quebec Act: extended the Canadian borders to reduce some of Massachusetts, Connecticut, and Virginia and removed all restrictions on the Catholic Church. It also denied the people the elected legislative assembly. The new oath of allegiance was now free of references to both the Protestant and Catholic faith.

Suffolk County demanded the shutting of the Boston Port. And the revoking of the October 1691 Massachusetts Charter. This had taken away the rights of the Massachusetts and Plymouth authorities to self-govern. Massachusetts also called for the establishment of a militia. Their actions would start a wave of resistance that grew across the colony.

At the second Continental Congress meeting on June 14, 1775, they decided to form a 'Continental Army'. Each colony would be allowed to raise a 'Continental Line' of regiments.

With the coming of the Revolutionary War, which side should be supported? Every family and adult in the thirteen colonies had to decide where to declare their allegiance. In the coming days, many people had to leave their homes and their country of birth. Those who called for independence called themselves 'Patriots'.

As mentioned, citizens who supported the Crown were known as 'Tories'. In the New York Journal of February 9, 1775, they quoted this answer to the question:

> "What is a Tory? 'A Tory is a thing whose head is in England, and its body in America, and its neck ought to be stretched."

These strong words and deep feelings would split families in the years to come. Disagreements would break out between fathers, mothers, brothers, cousins, and friends.

All Americans had to choose whether to remain loyal subjects to Great Britain and become a traitor to the United States or be a U.S. citizen and a traitor to the Crown.

Philip expanded his estates with the purchase in 1775 of more woodland and an additional farm on a branch of the Passaic River. There was a small pearl-ash factory near Pompton with woodland and meadow and the 'right of the bridge'. They produced pearl ash by treating wood and then potash baked in kilns. The final compound used a soluble white salt to make glass and ceramics. Some products produced were shipped to Great Britain.

Philip planned to move his buildings and build a barn on the new farm. He intended to design gardens down to the river and border them with tall oaks. In his plans, he proposed to lay out a spacious garden around the main house, complete with an ornamental island, a pond, and spreading beech trees.

With all these new buildings and the factory, Philip employed over fifty local workers on his farm.

Tensions were rising, and Philip had a visit from the local militia. They were under orders to confiscate two muskets and belts from him. The Rebels knew Philip's Tory views, as they had been monitoring him.

Later, in 1776, he had more visits to his house, and by order of Congress, they took away window leads, clock weights and other lead items. The new Continental Army needed these items so they could melt them down and construct badly needed weapons. Philip received a receipt for £71, but no payment.

****

4 LOYALTY

Philip, a dynamic academic and businessman, considered himself an American but agreed with his contemporaries that the British had poorly governed the colonies.

There was a need for change. Philip wished Americans could achieve this through negotiation with the British government. His strict Protestant background and his father's influence made him loyal to the Crown and the Empire. Like his fellow Loyalists, Philip agreed that the British Parliament was "the grand legislature of the Empire." He was resolute that he would not take up arms against the British government.

The clerical leader of the Loyalists was Dr Myles Cooper. At the time, the President of King's College. He reminded his fellow Americans that "God established the laws of government, ordained the British power and commanded all to obey authority." He also said that threatening open disrespect to the government was "an unpardonable crime."

It did not mean that Dr Cooper agreed with the Stamp Act of March 1765. This had imposed taxes on all legal and official papers and publications circulating in the colonies. This tariff had to be paid in British sterling, not colonial currency, which further irritated the people.

In fact, Dr Cooper stated it was contrary to American rights since the occupation of New Netherlands by the British.

Anglicanism in the colony and its teachings shaped and influenced general and political thinking. Philip's forward path was clear to him.

Although he came from one of the wealthiest and most prominent families in New York. The books written about the Loyalist cause rarely mention Philip.

Even in some military journals published, there is barely any reference to his service in the various units in which he served. He was not a great military leader of men or a war hero.

Philip believed in the possibility of independence for the American people. So, in 1775, as an elected deputy representing Westchester County, he met with other delegates.

They were to appoint members to the Continental Congress. He thought they could achieve positive change through negotiation and not by war.

Some representatives who attended the First Continental Congress were John and Samuel Adams from Massachusetts Bay, Peyton Randolph, who was elected president of the convention, and George Washington from Virginia. After seven weeks of debate, Congress approved plans to boycott British goods as a sign of protest. They also agreed to hold another congress meeting in May of the following year.

At the outbreak of war, the population of the colonies was approximately 2.5 million people.

Fighting broke out with the first battles of the Revolutionary War at Lexington and Concord on April 19, 1775, and so started a train of unstoppable events. Ninety-three Americans lost their lives or were wounded, with three hundred British troops killed, wounded, missing or captured. Over 5,460 men were involved in the battle, with victory to the Americans.

Trouble had been brewing since the British parliament passed the Stamp Act of 1763. The Reverend John Wiswall of Falmouth, New England, said, "even silence is now censured by the people as evidence of what they call Tory principles."

Times were changing, and there was much discontent in the colonies.

An inflammatory fifty-page pamphlet named 'Common Sense', written by a radical Englishman, Thomas Paine, in January 1776, advocating America's severing ties with the Mother Country, added fuel to the fire.

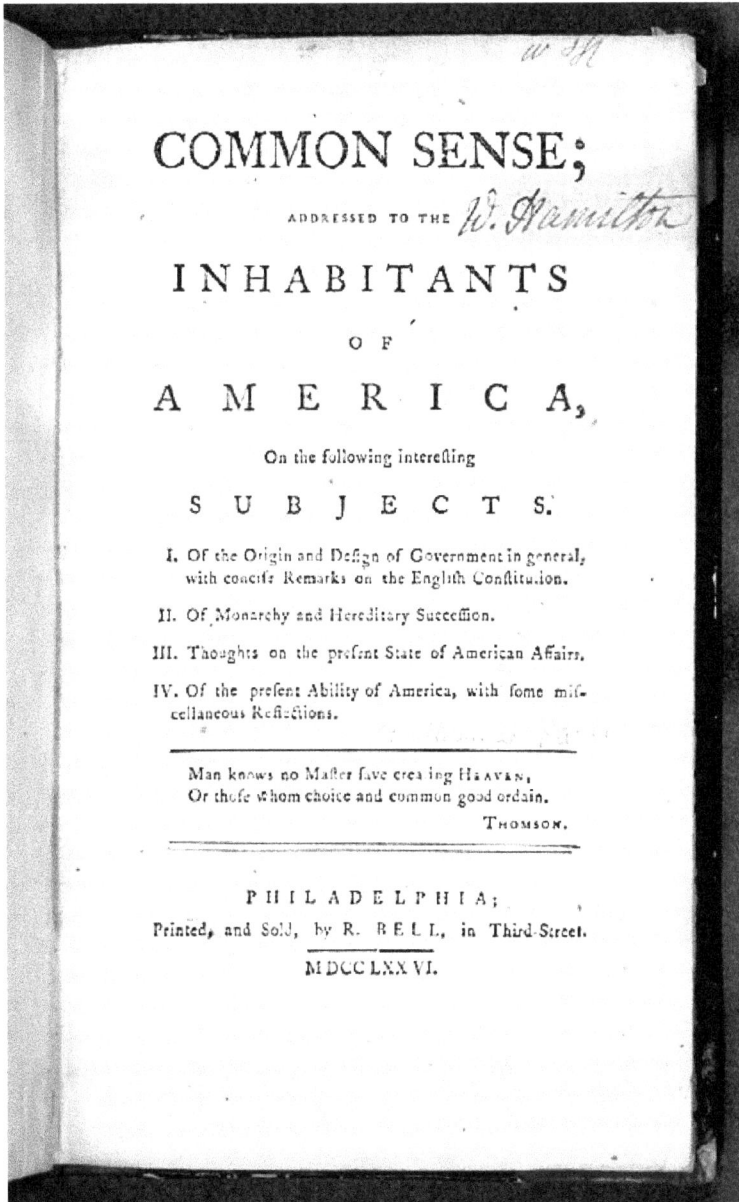

COMMON SENSE;

ADDRESSED TO THE *W. Hamilton*

INHABITANTS

O F

A M E R I C A,

On the following interesting

S U B J E C T S.

I. Of the Origin and Design of Government in general, with concise Remarks on the English Constitution.

II. Of Monarchy and Hereditary Succession.

III. Thoughts on the present State of American Affairs.

IV. Of the present Ability of America, with some miscellaneous Reflections.

Man knows no Master save creaing Heaven,
Or those whom choice and common good ordain.
THOMSON.

P H I L A D E L P H I A;
Printed, and Sold, by R. BELL, in Third-Street.
MDCCLXXVI.

Paine, who was born in January 1737, grew up in Thetford, England. As a young adult, he moved to Sussex and became an excise inspector. During the six years he lived in the town, he travelled around, where he used to proclaim his "revolutionary theories" in the taverns in Lewes.

After a chance meeting with Benjamin Franklin in London in November 1774, Paine travelled to Philadelphia. There, he found employment with the Pennsylvania Magazine.

A few years later, Paine returned to England, where he wrote another controversial publication called 'Rights of Man' (1791). This book defended the French Revolution.

Britain banned the book, and the authorities indicted Paine for treason, but he fled to France. His outspoken writings caused offence in France, and for a year, they imprisoned him. Paine stayed in France until 1802, when he returned to the United States. He died in Greenwich Village, New York City, on June 8, 1809.

Later, John Adams (1735-1826), the second President of the United States, wrote:

"Without the pen of the author of 'Common Sense,' the sword of Washington would have been raised in vain,"

In 1969, the United States Post Office Department, in its series of Prominent Americans, issued a 40c stamp with the portrait of Thomas Paine. There is also a statue in Morristown's Burnham Park, Morris County, N.J., acknowledging Thomas Paine. Also, a monument in New Rochelle, New York, and another in Thetford, Norfolk, England. In 2010, the town of Lewes unveiled a statue that had been sculpted by local artist Marcus Cornish.

The Continental Army entered New York City and started either expelling or arresting Loyalists.

Patriots hounded, robbed, beat, and forced Tories out of town. There were also some extreme cases of tar and feathering of Loyalists.

On April 28, 1775, the records show Philip being a judge in Morris County. Still, his and his family's lives were about to change forever.

Morris County committee held a meeting on May 1, 1775, and they agreed to "raise men, money and arms for the common defence."

Trouble was looming, and the officers of the Morris County Militia held a general meeting in June 1775. The meeting took place at the house of Captain Peter Dickinson, the tavern keeper in Morristown.

They proposed that there should be a mass resignation of the militia officers. All present at the meeting agreed except for Philip, who vehemently opposed their conclusions. He later sent his fellow officers a letter imploring them to reconsider their plan to resign their commissions and to stay loyal to the king.

Philip stated he would not follow their example and set out his reasons. He explained that they should make all their decisions calmly and wait for the outcome of the Continental Congress to conclude a peaceful solution to the troubles. He suggested that any momentous decision could have grave consequences. Philip then declared his devotion to the Corps and the welfare of his country.

Philip sent a letter 'To the Officers of the Militia of the County of Morris assembled at Morris Town on Friday, 15th June 1775'[17].

Hanover, 12th June 1775

Gentlemen

Being informed that a meeting of the Officers of the Militia in the

---

[17] TNA, AO 13/54/631-632

County of Morris is proposed to be held at Morris Town on Friday next for the purpose of considering of the propriety of resigning the Commissions they hold over Government, & lest I should be prevented from attending said meeting, would wish to communicate to you my sentiments on the subject with that freedom which I think the importance of the occasion justly merits & which as an English Subject I am entitled to express.

Permit me Gentlemen to entreat you to proceed on this

business with the greatest caution & circumspection, to act with such prudence on this Solemn occasion that the World may see that your deperminations are the result of calm deliberation becoming men who are contending for their liberty's upon the Solid principles of that happy Constitution which is the birth right & boast of Englishmen & the envy & admiration of all the World. The Continental Congress is now sitting & the united wisdom of this Country is supposed to be collected, with a view to adopt some plan for the preservation of American freedom & to settle the unhappy dispute with our mother Country upon an equitable & lasting foundation.

Let us not therefore Gentlemen Counteract their labours by our hasty resolutions especially in a matter of so momentuous consequence--but wait the result of their proceedings with a little patience, conducrt ourselves with discretion which will ensure success in every undertaking.

I cannot think the resignation proposed can have any good tendency, but may be productive of bad consequences, tho' should I in this opinion be so unfortunate as to differ with my brother Officers, I hope you will treat with tenderness an honest zeal which I assure you is devoted to the honor of the Corps of which I am a member, & to the happiness & welfare of my Country in whose just defence I would endeavour to be among its foremost advocates.

I am with great esteem

Gentlemen

Your Most Obedt. huml. Servt.

P[hilip] V[AN] C[ORTLAND]

In June 1775, Philip's 'Memorandum Book' records his feelings.

AMERICA TROUBLES COMMENCE

"The Officers of the Militia for the County of Morris have a General meeting at the house of Peter Dickinson tavern keeper & agree to resign their Commissions under Government… which that all did except myself who could not be convinced of the propriety of the measure & therefore gave reasons in writing for dissenting from them in opinion called upon to appear in Arms by order of the Coll. But would not comply notwithstanding very severe threats on the occasion"-

Not long after this meeting, the participants contacted Philip regarding a proposal they had received from Congress. They requested that he convert his pearl ash manufacturing business into nitre works. They informed Philip that this was to aid the colonial war effort.

Philip refused to do this, even though they promised him high profits for his work. This matter was not finished as soon after they offered Philip a commission in the American army with an assurance of fast promotion.

Philip declined this proposal. His refusal did not endear him to his fellow officers.

These fellow officers in the militia later formed the first revolutionary military company in Morris County.

Philip was a New Yorker and descended from a wealthy and privileged family.

He had only recently had the family moved to Whippany. Philip identified himself and his family as Loyalists. The family understood and sympathised with the American claims of injustice, but they would stay loyal to the British crown.

Hanover Township and the surrounding area were rich in iron ore. Mining companies had mined ore there since the early 1700s. Before that, the indigenous Indians had mined the ore.

In 1750, the British government passed a law prohibiting Americans from smelting iron ore into pig iron or flat sheets.

They had to send their untreated ore to England for processing. This ruling angered the local people and helped cultivate strong revolutionary feelings in the county. But it did not stop the illicit workings of the iron ore.

The postal service was another area for aggrievement. Mail between the colonies had first to be sent to government offices in London before being brought back to America. Only people with the means could afford private messengers to deliver their mail.

It was not until July 1775, and after the Second Continental Congress, that the colonies had a regular and reliable mail service. They elected Benjamin Franklin as the first Postmaster General. From 1753 to 1774, as joint Postmaster General, he oversaw Britain's colonial mail service and helped to improve a courier service that connected the thirteen colonies, setting up an effective postal network. He later standardised shipping rates, which were based on weight and distance, thereby enhancing the efficiency of postal operations.

In the following days, Philip travelled to the south and met with fellow-minded Loyalists. Philip was so enraged by some church ministers' actions and their speeches against the Crown that he started distributing Loyalist pamphlets.

His memoir entry under 1775 quotes:

"in order to escape the furious patriots of Jersey whose zeal

has been worked up to a high pitch of
enthusiasm by the continued lectures of their pious
Presbyterian priests, who were indefatigable in the
good Cause. During my absence I had frequent
opportunities of being in Company & conversing with
the gentlemen who composed the Southern
Committees". "They declared their design in filling
ev'ry publick office was to keep power out of the hands
of the lower class of people."

In the New York Journal of June 1, they carried details of the General Committee of Association meeting. They held this in Newark, New Jersey. The Committee directed its address to the deputies elected to represent the town in the Provincial Congress.

Philip Van Cortlandt and Isaac Ogden were among the deputies. This was a call to arms and the appointment of general committees. They were to organise volunteers, with commanders and field officers.

In England, an article appeared in a provincial newspaper about Philip: 17 July 1775 — Chester Chronicle — Chester, Cheshire, England.

Fled to Pennsylvania and Maryland after talking his
way out of arrest. Then returned to New Jersey, where
he was fined and forbidden to carry arms.

Locally, some Loyalists were treated very badly, as this article from Georgia shows[18].

My Lord, on the 24th instant [of this month] about 9 o'clock at Night I heard a very great Huzzaing in the Streets, and on Sending out found

---

they had seized upon one Hopkins, a Pilot, and were Tarring and Feathering him, and Soon after they brought him in a Cart along by my House and such a Horrid Spectacle I really never Saw. They made the Man Stand up in a Cart with a Candle in his Hand and a great many Candles were Carried round the Cart and thus they went through most of the Streets in town for upwards of three Hours. And on Inquiring what he had done, I was Informed that he had behaved disrespectfully towards the Sons of Liberty and Drank some Toasts which gave great offense, but for Your Lordship's more Particular Information in both these Matters I enclose a Copy of the Affidavits of the Parties and the Newspaper, and I must at the same time observe that I cannot believe this Conduct is Promoted or Approved of by the People in General, but only by some very Violent ones amongst them and the Mob. Your Lordship will be the best Judge what is most Proper to be done, but I beg leave again most heartily to wish that Conciliatory Measures may Speedily take place or total Ruin and Destruction will soon follow, and America Lost and Gone.

___ Sir James Wright, governor of Georgia, part of the letter to Lord Dartmouth, 29 July 1775,

The Town Committee at Morristown summoned Philip's cousin, Cortlandt Skinner (16 December 1727–15 March 1799), before them in September 1775.

Cortlandt Skinner was an outspoken family member and the son of Elizabeth (Van Cortlandt) Skinner, Philip's aunt. He worked as a lawyer and became Speaker of the House of Assembly during the years 1765-1770 and 1772-1776.

After Governor Jonathan Belcher's appointment, he served as New Jersey Attorney General from 1754 until the outbreak of hostilities between England and the colonies in 1776.

At the committee meeting, Philip spoke passionately on his behalf.

He defended his cousin's good nature, strong Christian beliefs, and compassion for his fellow American citizens. But to no avail, as the Committee found Cortlandt Skinner guilty of being ill-disposed to the liberties of America.

Still, the Committee considered Philip's pleas on behalf of his cousin, and they discharged him. No further charges or fines were brought against Cortlandt Skinner.

After the Committee had concluded its meeting, Philip helped escort his cousin to return home safely.

In March 1786, Cortlandt Skinner wrote to the Claims Memorials Committee in London. He supported Philip's claim for compensation.[19] Cortlandt conveyed the details of this episode, which took place in 1775 in Morristown to the Claims Committee.

In the meantime, Catherine had another son born in Hanover in September 1775. He was their third son, whom they named Richard Willing. Unfortunately, he died on March 16, 1778, aged two years and six months, after surviving the family journey from Hanover.

The church burial records show the family buried Richard in Grace Church Cemetery in Jamaica, Queens County.

It must have been devastating for the family, as so far, only one of their sons has survived to become a young man.

In December 1775, Philip wrote to his friend and former classmate Isaac Wilkins, who was in London. He advised him that the situation in New York was changing, with the streets full of armed Republicans.

His friend from Westchester was born in Withywood, Jamaica, in December 1742. They had both attended King's College and remained in contact over the years.

---

[19] TNA, AO13/54/653

Isaac had been a representative in the State Colonial Assembly from 1768 until 1775. In February 1775, he gave a speech to the General Assembly in New York, urging reconciliation with Britain.

This is an extract from his speech.

> "The necessity of a speedy reconciliation between us and our mother country must be obvious to everyone who is not totally destitute of sense and feeling."[20]

He also wrote many pamphlets supporting the British and the monarchy. Some of these appeared in the 'Westchester Farmer.' A collection of pamphlets published in Westchester, New York, by the Reverend Samuel Seabury (1729-1796) to support the Loyalists' argument against American independence from Britain.

Isaac did not want to fight in the war and addressed the newly formed Provincial Congress on May 3, 1775. Part of this was the following statement.

> "I leave America, and every endearing connection, because I will not raise my hand against my Sovereign, nor will I draw my sword against my country – when I can conscientiously draw it in her favour, my life shall be cheerfully devoted to her service."

The Committee issued the following notice on 5 May.

---

[20] "Address to the New York Assembly, Debates, 23 February 1775," 1, *American Archives*, at 1295.

TO THE
PEOPLE OF AMERICA.

Stop him! Stop him! Stop him!
One Hundred Pounds Lawful Money Reward!

A WOLF in Sheep's Clothing!

A TRAITOR!

WHEREAS ISAAC WILKINS, of the Province of New-York, has made his escape from the place of his former residence, after having betrayed the confidence of his constituents, and villanously consented, that they, and their posterity, should become abject Slaves, to the mercenary, and tyrannical Parliament of Great-Britain ; and hath, in divers other instances, endeavoured to destroy the Liberties of America, in which ▆▆▆ Freedom will reign amidst the most sanguinary machinations of her inveterate enemies.——Therefore, whoever apprehends the said Isaac Wilkins, and secures him, that he may be sent to the Provincial Camp, in Massachusetts-Bay, shall receive the above reward, of the Commanding Officer of the said camp.

By order of the committee.

NEW-LONDON. May 4. 1775.

21

After his speech, he left New York with his wife, Isabella, the daughter of Colonel Lewis Morris, whom he had married in November 1762.

The family with eight children travelled to England. Times changed, and Isaac decided to return to Long Island in the summer of 1776, where he stayed until the end of hostilities.

He sold his family's lands and farm at Castle Hill Neck for £2,500 in New York Currency, half of his original payment for the property.

---

[21] Retrieved from the Library of Congress, https://www.loc.gov/item/2002705577/.

When the British government, after the conflict, allocated him an allowance of one hundred and twenty pounds for life and lands in Nova Scotia, he departed America.

So, in 1783, Isaac joined the journey to Shelburne, Nova Scotia. Later, he joined the judiciary as the First Judge of the Court of Common Pleas and became prominent in the town and its development. After eleven years in Nova Scotia, he returned to Westchester and took Anglican orders. He became rector of St. Peter's Church in Westchester Village of the Bronx in New York on March 9, 1799, a position he held until his death on February 5, 1830.

Philip wrote to his friend in London.

Hanover, 7th December 1775[22]

Dear WILKINS

In what terms to address you at this juncture I
am at a loss & must candidly acknowledge my
inability to the temper of the times, I dare not
speak, think, or even dream, how then can I write,
& especially to the friend of my bosom? with whom,
but lately the least appearance of reserve would have
been criminal? Gracious heavens!
To what a situation are we reduced- not many months ago
did we boast of our happy condition in enjoying every earthly
felicity in this new World than even the most extravagant
fancy could suggest- the tree of peace seemed to have taken
deep root in our fertile soil- our Commerse

---

[22] TNA. AO13. Volume 54. Folio 633-4.

extending to every known part of the habitable
Globe, furnishing us with all the necessarys nay
luxurys of life- the Sciences were introduced
respected & courted- in Short nothing seemed
wanting to conspire to make us a flourishing great &
happy people but our own knowledge of it &
gratitude to all bountiful heaven for our happy
Situation-

how Alas is the scene changed-the streets of our
once thriving City that used to throng with the
produce of Europe & both the Indias are now filled
with the Goods & effects of its deserting inhabitants
& instead of the gay & pleasing appearance of our
blooming females we have the glittering of Musketts
Swords & bayonets under the banners of Rebellion-
but Stop I am going too far.

Yesterday being the first leisure time since the
increase of my flock I made an Attempt in
Company with the two Doctors of Jamaica to pay a
visit to Castle Hill-

after waiting 'till sunset at Abraham's we were
obliged to return as our signal was not observed, it
being somewhat blustering, tho' I had the pleasure
to hear that your dear Isa & little ones were all well
the day before, this I had from the Coll. whose wife
has made him a father as well as a husband.

Present my best regards to the worthy Doctor of
Kings, tell him it will afford me great pleasure to
have a line from him-
do not forget my Sincerest respects to the Revd.

& Capt. late of Shrewsbury in Monmouth New Jersey, they can tell you many things-

& by all means remember me to the Doctor of Elizabeth & the Revd. John of Kings, let the latter know that I am almost convinced of the old proverb, how happy should I be to smoke one social pipe with you all, but that must be deferr'd to a future day, & when that day will arrive neither of us knows.

Our worthy & deservedly esteemed Governor TRYON is soon to leave us to the great regret of every friend to this Country, indeed the Province must sustain an irraparable loss as the whole of his conduct during his administration justly entitles him to the character of a wise Legislator humane Judge and worthy Citizen.

I had the pleasure of spending a day last week with the venerable old Lieut. Governor at his seat- he is in as perfect health & intelects as twenty years past without the least variation, but am apt to conclude he would rather spend his remaining Glass in his peacefull retirement on Nassau Island.

'Tis now time to finish & bid you Adieu perhaps (ay perhaps my dear Isaac) for ever-may the King of Kings gaurd us both & ever remind us of the Concius recti: farewell again & may you be happy is the sincere wish of

Your Affectionate friend

P[hilip] V[AN] C[ORTLAND]

N.B.- This is my fourth letter unanswered.

New York's provincial legislature was holding a meeting in early 1776, and after Philip attended, he wrote:

"Committee of Senators with all the marks of wisdom which
flapt hats, large caps & black short pipes could give
them"."a puritanical, hipocritical-Weaver chosen
Councillor" "Tavern keepers of Sage Understanding
chosen Assemblymen" "a drunken, canting Deacon well
known in the broad Alley for repeated offenses" he
then noted "A most respectable group!"

Rhode Island was the first American colony to renounce allegiance to King George III on May 4, 1776.

On June 7, 1776, the Continental Congress held a meeting in Philadelphia. At this meeting, Richard Henry Lee of Virginia presented his submission, the "Lee Motion", which was seconded by John Adams. In it, he stated:

"That these United Colonies are, and of right out to be, free and
independent States, that they are absolved from all allegiance to the
British Crown, and that all political connection between them and the
State of Great Britain is, and ought to be, totally dissolved; that
measures should be immediately taken for procuring the assistance of
foreign powers, and a Confederation be formed to bind the colonies
more closely together."

This meeting adjourned, but at the Second Continental Congress meeting on July 2, 1776, Philadelphia voted for independence. Also, on the 2nd, New Jersey adopted a constitution declaring independence from Great Britain. They were the fourth American colony to do so.

Although signed on the 2nd, on July 4 , Congress approved the final text of the Declaration and made a formal announcement. Loyalists were now considered traitors.

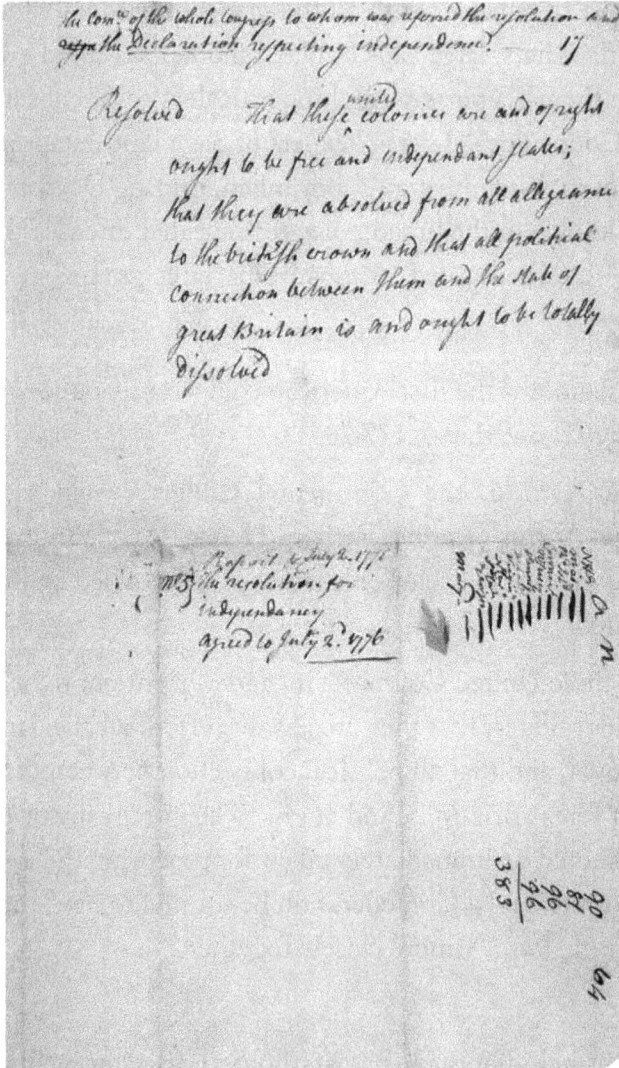

Adoption of the Resolution Calling for Independence from England; 7/2/1776; [23]

[23] Reports on Administrative Affairs of the Congress; Papers of the Continental Congress, 1774-1789; Records of the Continental and Confederation Congresses and the Constitutional Convention, Record Group 360; National Archives Building, Washington, DC.

At the meeting of the fourth New York Provincial Congress at White Plains on July 9. The chairman, Nathaniel Woodhull, and delegates received a copy of the recent resolution passed by the Continental Congress. It was the "Declaration of Independence".

Constitution   Wynn Pointaux

New York had been waiting for this news and passed a resolution approving the declaration.

Congress also informed them of recent developments. They advised that on July 2 at 8 p.m., British troops had taken possession of Staten Island without opposition from the residents. They warned that detachments of British soldiers had advanced towards Bergen Point and Elizabeth Town.

This news marked the beginning of a three-year campaign by the revolutionary leadership of New York State.

They decided they would identify, separate, and expel Loyalists who did not support the republican cause for independence. They also singled out citizens who wished to remain neutral.

However, it was not until September 3, 1783, after the signing of the Treaty of Paris and the formal ending of the war, that the northern states were independent.

The actions of Congress would have a life-changing effect on Philip and his family. In his memoir, he wrote

"July 4th Independency Declared

The Congress having reason to conclude from the temper of their subjects that if proposals any ways favourable should be offer'd on the part of Great Britain they would accept- most industriously by their Preachers hold up the idea of nothing but absolute unconditional submission on their part- which with great artifice is circulated thro. the Country in order to prepare the deluded people for the declaration of their darling Idol. Independency- which a few weeks before they had reprobated...."

The Chairman of the County Committee, Alexander Carmichael, called a meeting at County Hall, Morris County, in August 1776. Where they filed a formal complaint against Philip for not bearing arms.

Again, they advised Philip to join the militia or pay a man to take his place, as it was acceptable at this time, but Philip's reply was robust with the words:

"could a substitute be procured for the tenth part of a farthing, I would not send one, as I should look upon him as my representitive, and therefore accountable for his conduct — at the same time that I looked upon this

treatment as cruel ungenerous, and incompatible with
my notions of liberty."

He admitted the offence and stated:

"that the prospect of loosing property & life would never induce me
to draw my Sword against my Sovereign, & no tortures they could
inflict should ever influence me to change my principles."

The committee acquitted Philip on the condition that he behaved himself, was friendly to the cause of freedom, and assisted the American States and Congress.

After this meeting, Philip travelled to Pennsylvania and Maryland before returning to New Jersey.

Soon after, the committee issued orders that forbade Philip from carrying any weapons. The reason given was that they had repeatedly fined him for not taking up arms against His Majesty's armies. Philip had refused, and the records show that on September 3, 1776, he had paid a fine of £3.0.0. This was for not carrying arms against His Majesty's fleets and armies.

Moses Fairchild, born in 1748 in Hanover, Morris, New Jersey, whom Philip had employed for the previous two years, signed Philip's receipt.

Philip later produced copies of these for the Claims and Memorials in London as further evidence of his treatment by the colonialists.

Claims and Memorials [24]

In Committee of the County of Morris Augt. 7th 1776

---

[24] TNA. AO13, Volume 54, folio 636

A Complaint being formily made against Capt. Philip CORTLANDT for not bearing Arms and he being cited to appear before this board, he accordingly appeared & confessed the Charge and this Committee having well considered said Charge do acquit him from the same he behaving himself for the future friendly to the Cause of freedom & the American States and assisting in every other measure agreable to the Rules of Congress and in Case he should in future be allotted to go in the Service he shall accept of the same or hire a man in his Room.

Extract from the minutes.

Alexdr. Carmichael   Chairman

Receipt for Payment of a Fine[25]

Received Hanover 3rd September 1776 from Philip Van Cortland the sum of three pounds proclamation money in full for a fine imposed on him agreable to a resolve of the Provincial Congress for refusing to bear arms against his Majesty's fleets and armies, he having been detached for said service on Monday the 12th day of August past, received in behalf and by order of Capt. Obadiah Kitchel -

Moses Fairchild   £3. 0. 0. Proc.

Philip noted in his memoir that Moses Fairchild had been employed in his service for two years and "preserved from staving."

On September 15, 1776, the British forces captured New York City. Where they stayed until hostilities ceased in 1783.

The American Council of Safety, at their meeting on September 19, 1776, introduced a law that civilians and military personnel had to sign. It said,

---

[25] TNA. AO13, Volume 54. folio 639.

"I do sincerely profess and swear [or affirm] that I do and will bear true Faith and Allegiance to the Government established in this State, under the Authority of the People … I do sincerely profess and swear [or affirm] that I do not hold myself bound to bear allegiance to the King of Great Britain. So help me God."

The new British commander-in-chief, General William Howe (1729-1814), who had recently taken over from Major General Thomas Gage (1721-1787), planned and led the attack on Staten Island.

The government in Great Britain had replaced General Gage. They recalled him to London after his disastrous management of the 1775 Lexington campaign. The first major battle of the American Revolution in which the British, who were outnumbered two to one in the fight, suffered three hundred casualties compared to the ninety-three American ones. Round one to the Revolutionaries.

General Gage had spent most of his life in America. And invested in land in New York State. Although he was a British General commanding the troops against the American cause, the new authorities did not confiscate any of his lands. Unlike the outcome for other prominent landowning Loyalists.

When the British took control of New York City in August, they had problems with the housing of over six thousand rebel prisoners. The British urgently required accommodations to house them in the city.

Martial law was imposed on the city, and the military forced the local authorities to use private buildings to house prisoners. Warehouses like the Rhinelander Sugar House at Rose and Duane Streets, and churches were also used as temporary prisons. Later, to ease the situation, the British used prison ships to contain prisoners.

With the British now in charge, there were hostilities at first. The treatment of the city's residents at the beginning was no better than when the republicans occupied the city. But soon the situation settled down, and life improved for the townsfolk.

Before the start of hostilities, Phillip's neighbours had been good friends but were now turning against the family.

As the situation changed, Philip took his young children out of school as they were receiving abuse and insults from the other children.

In his memoir, he noted: "with sobs & tears on account of abuse from the inhuman wretches."[26] Even the family dog, Beaver, was attacked, and they had left him for dead. Beaver went missing for two days until, eventually, the family found him tied to a tree with a leash.

The injured poor animal had received numerous cuts and bruises, and they found him with one of his eyes hanging down his cheek. But the dog survived with much love and great care from the family.

Philip recorded in his memoir in November 1776, "the truly pious Revd. Mr. Chapman" at a recent meeting urged his congregation to turn out and fight "those plunderers of their Country." and "that evr'y one who fell in battle would be translated into heaven."

Shortly after General Charles Lee (1731-1782) and his army arrived in Morris County, they issued an arrest warrant for Philip's capture. It was on the orders of General Washington (1732-1799).

Morris County played an essential role during the Revolutionary War. It was also the winter headquarters for Washington's forces.

The county, situated just thirty miles west of New York City, became the Continental Army's military capital from 1777 to 1780. It was General George Washington's headquarters. And one of the winter quarters for his troops.

During the insurrection, Morris County did not have any battles or any intrusion from British forces.

Whilst visiting his great aunt, Mrs Gertrude Beekman, Philip received a message from a young boy.

---

[26] Philip's memoir entry dated 2 September 1776.

Some friends had sent the boy through the woods to advise Philip that a friend of his had just been detained.

The message said that Philip's imminent arrest was possible within the hour. Philip had travelled on his favourite horse, Samson, to visit his aunt and departed for home at once.

General Lee arrived in Morristown on December 8, 1776, with an advance guard and a detachment of Light Horse cavalry. These were hastily dispatched to Philip's aunt's house to arrest him. Their orders were to detain him and escort him to Easton with his horse, Samson.

General Lee had met Philip a little while ago and admired his horse, Samson. This was an opportunity for him to acquire the horse.

With good fortune on his side, Philip escaped these troops with minutes to spare and departed for home and then to his cousin Cortlandt Skinner, in New York City, for refuge.

Catharine's idyllic and comfortable life was about to be shattered by the following events. Her republican neighbours rose against the family, and it would be three months before the family reunited with Philip again.

Philip wrote in his memoir on 8 December 1776.

"Notwithstanding my feelings at the thoughts of leaving
my family consisting of twenty-four in number among whom a
beloved Wife and nine children. From all happiness to be exiled, either
voluntarily or by the hand of lawless usurpation of power was a
determination soon made. However severe the conflict – whilst my
horse was coming to the door I passed thro' my house. Looked at my
children who with my dr. wife were gazing at me – I could no more.
But rode off -."

The journey was dangerous, with Philip taking refuge in the mountains whilst being pursued by rebel Light Horse cavalry. He eventually met up with the British army on the Newark Road.

Philip arrived in New York City on 8 December 1776 with a broken heart, leaving his beloved Kitty, nine children, and fourteen staff at home. Philip did not realise that he would never return to Hanover and relax in his large, comfortable home again.

His journey was difficult, with many narrow escapes from capture by his pursuers. This is part of Philip's account of his journey:

"Mountains, December 8th., 1776. About eleven o'clock at night, after a fatiguing ride thro' bye road and totally absent in thought I had made a circuitous jaunt of 30 miles and had gained 5 from home, by which means fell

in with Lee's Army at Troy and had nearly got half way into their cantonment before I perceived my error — was obliged to make use of a Stratagem to get clear, which happily (tho' with difficulty) effected — took a different rout and got safe to Boonton — received information that two party's of Light horse had been at my house within ten minutes after my departure and had fix'd a gaurd."

Philip had taken some family silver with him, which he later sold in New York.

Before leaving his farm, Philip entrusted his Dutch neighbours with his prize cows for safekeeping. Still, later, colonial soldiers found and slaughtered them.

By mid-December, Philip was dining with General William Howe (1729-1814) in New York City. He visited General James Robertson (1717-1788), the civil governor of the Province of New York.

James Robertson was the city's 40th governor, serving from March 1780 until April 1783. He questioned Philip's motives for being in New York. General Robertson's attitude perplexed Philip. This dissuaded him from taking up a military commission.

Later in New Jersey, Philip called upon Governor William Franklin (1730-1813). Where Philip noted, "where the conversation & reception were so differen." The governor offered him the rank of Lieutenant-Colonel and requested him to raise a brigade of Loyalists.

Philip then contacted his cousin, now Brigadier General[27] Cortlandt Skinner, who was a commander with the British troops.

The British referred to the American Tory units as the Loyalist Provincial Corps.

On September 4, 1776, they appointed Philip's cousin Commander of the New Jersey Volunteers. Under the previous administration, Cortlandt Skinner had been the 7th Royal Attorney General of New Jersey, serving from 1754 to 1776. He was also a past speaker of the New Jersey General Assembly. Cortlandt actively opposed American independence.

Like his cousin Philip, the colonialists had offered Cortlandt Skinner choice positions in the Patriot American military. But like Philip, he declined to take up arms against the Crown.

It was, of course, after friends had informed Philip in December 1776 of an intercepted letter and that the Rebels had authorised his arrest, that he fled to New York.

He and his cousin thought of themselves as Americans. They had supported the Colonial cause, but not how they chose to obtain their goals. Both men were highly educated and from very privileged backgrounds. They had hoped to negotiate a reasonable settlement with the British government.

Unfortunately, they both were out of touch with the wave of independence demanded by their fellow citizens. Subsequently, they both served in the British Army until the end of hostilities and then fled to England.

---

[27] Cortland Skinner commissioned as Brigadier General TNA. AO 13. Volume 108. Folio 276,

Within ten minutes of Philip's departure from Dashwood, a party of rebel Light Horsemen headed by Captain Joseph Morris arrived at his house to arrest him.

One soldier said that although they had much esteem for the family, General Lee had said that Philip was "as one too dangerous to be permitted to stay in the county." So, they had their duty to do. After questioning his family, the soldiers departed.

They placed an armed guard outside his home and, in the days that followed, regularly searched the house for him. The following day, another group of soldiers arrived with a document from General Lee for Philip to swear to. The officers quoted some words that General Lee had said:

"he had drawn up himself in the most tender terms, as he had formerly received many civilities from your family and respected your character."

Again, the soldiers questioned the family and servants, who denied any knowledge of Philip's whereabouts.

To capture Philip, the Horsemen surrounded the house with twenty armed men every night. They also placed a soldier by the front gate during the day, hoping to catch him on his return.

Philip's wife, Catharine, sent a letter on 15 December 1776. This was advising him of the terrible ordeal she and the family were suffering. Catharine wrote four letters during those weeks, describing the events she and the children endured and their perilous journey to New York, where the family were eventually reunited with Philip.

Extract of Catherine's letter dated 15 December 1776.[28]

My dearest love,

You had not left us ten minutes last Sunday when a party of Light Horsemen, headed by Joseph Morris, came to our once peaceful mansion all armed, who said they had positive orders to take you,

my dear Philly, prisoner to Easton, and your favorite horse Sampson to be carried to Morristown for the use of General Lee from whom these cruel mandates were issued.

What were my emotions on seeing these wretches alight and without ceremony enter the doors you can only conceive,

you who know

their base characters and how their present errand must be received by your beloved family.

When these bloody minded men came into the dining room, our little flock gathered around me and with anxious eyes watched my looks, whilst I was answering questions respecting your eluding their search.

One of them (flourishing his sword) swore bitterly that, if you was to be found alive on earth, he would take you or have your heart's blood. This was too much. They fled into their nursery, bursting into tears; screams out, 'Oh my dear Pappa, they will kill him, they will kill him.'

One of the inhuman men seemed touched, and endeavoured an excuse by saying they were sent by their General and therefore were obliged to do their duty, even though against a person they formerly much esteemed, but had been represented to General Lee as one too dangerous to be permitted to stay in the country.

Finding you was certainly gone and no prospect of obtaining from

---

[28] Vernon-Jackson, H. O. H., "A Loyalist's Wife: Letters of Mrs Philip Van Cortlandt December 1776 to February 1777", *History Today Magazine*, Volume XIV, no. 8, Pages 574-580.

me your intended route or any intimation of your return,
they went off, and left me in a situation (from my great exertions)
scarce to be described.

My first care was the nursery to comfort those innocent pledges of
our mutual love. They would scarcely hear me; their sobbing and crying
had almost overcome them; and they would not be persuaded from a
belief that the wretches were gone to murder their dear Pappa.

The next day another party of horsemen came down; who brought
with them an oath for you to subscribe, which General Lee said 'he
had drawn up himself in the most tender terms, as he had formerly
received many civilities from your family and respected your character.

By the contents you may judge my answer, which was, that it
was impossible for me to tell where you was gone. That I was
confident you would never subscribe to such conditions, and
that I would rather endure every inconvenience from a
separation than see you return subject to their power. This
explanation seemed to chagrin them, and they left me

rather abruptly.

The house is surrounded by eighteen or twenty armed men
every night in expectation of intercepting you, as they observed
that you was too much attached to your family to be long
absent.

Our dear children are again taken from school in
consequence of the cruel insults they daily receive for the
principles of their parents. I now write in fear and trembling and
venture this by an honest Dutch farmer who says he will deliver
it into your hands

Here is a copy of the oath drawn up by General Lee for Philip Van Cortland to subscribe. This was to ensure his protection and permission to return to his family in the County of Morris in 1776.[29]

"I ……….. do most religiously and solemnly swear in the presence of Almighty God that I will not give or cause to be given to the King's Army or fleet, or to any Officers Civil or Military under him any intelegence of any kind, that I will not knowingly receive any letters or Messages from them, & that those I shall receive unknowingly shall be disclosed to the General Commanding the Continental Troops.

I do also swear that I will not by my conversation by hints or even insinuations or suggestions endeavours to slacken the Zeal of those who are embarked in the service of the United States for the preservation of American Rights.

And still more particularly I do swear, as I hope for eternal salvation, that I will not endeavour to encrease the number of the King's adherents."

Why General Lee and his officers thought Philip was such a dangerous threat and that they should arrest him immediately is a mystery. He was not gathering a private army or arms to fight the Colonials.

Although very outspoken and having distributed some Loyalist leaflets, Philip was carrying on with his rural life.

His farms and factory provided paid work for many of the residents in Whippany. Philip knew most of the militia's prominent members well and usually had good relations with them.

Philip's family at Cortlandt Manor were firm supporters of independence.

---

[29] TNA. AO13. Volume 54. folio.646.

So why did they and General Lee not try harder to persuade Philip to change his hostility toward the idea of American independence from Britain? The continuous harassment and ill-treatment of Philip and his family compelled him to consider joining the British Army. Now, circumstances beyond his control made him take up arms against his fellow citizens.

In a twist of fate, on December 13, 1776, an incident occurred. After gathering intelligence, a small British Light Horse platoon of about thirty men on a reconnaissance mission under Lieutenant Colonel William Harcourt's command captured General Charles Lee.

Lee was staying at White's Tavern, Basking Ridge, New Jersey, which was some three miles from his army encampment.

There are reports that when captured, the prisoner said, "Good God! What will Lord and General Howe do with me?"[30] This incident occurred just a few days after Philip joined the British army.

General Lee (1732-1782) was born in Darnhall, Cheshire, England. He served in the British army and first came to America in 1756 with his regiment. Because of a lack of promotion, Lee resigned his commission, relinquished his half-pay, and travelled to Europe. Where he joined the Polish army. On November 10, 1773, he returned to America. Lee was sympathetic to the republican cause, and after being offered a major-general's commission, he joined the Republican army.

The British later released General Lee under a prisoner exchange for General Richard Prescott in 1778. Led by Lieutenant-Colonel William Barton, in a daring night raid by the Americans on Prescott Farm, Middletown, Newport County, Rhode Island, on July 10, 1777, they captured General Prescott, who commanded the British-Hessian forces.

Shortly after General William Howe arrived on Staten Island on July 7, 1776, he appointed Cortlandt Skinner as colonel.

---

[30] The Chelmsford Chronicle, Friday, 28 February, 1777.

Soon after, Cortlandt received a promotion to Brigadier-General[31]. General Howe then requested him to organise and raise five battalions. They were to comprise two thousand and five hundred soldiers.

Cortlandt Skinner raised six companies.

There would eventually be over three thousand three hundred men serving in the New Jersey Volunteers. He was to appoint 'under the command of gentlemen of the country nominated by himself' as officers. Cortlandt Skinner became commander of the New Jersey Volunteers on September 4, 1776.

Staten Island is in the Bay of New York, close to the New Jersey shore. The island, 13.7 miles long and 8 miles wide, was first discovered by Giovanni De Verrazzano in 1524. He anchored offshore in his vessel *La Dauphine* for one night and did not explore this new land.

Later, Henry Hudson, in September 1609, arrived and spent a month exploring the island.

In 1636, David Pietersen de Vries (1593-1655), on August 13, received a grant for part of Staaten Eylandt. On arrival, he immediately built a block fort and signal station. Then he built huts near the fort to accommodate the soldiers and officials. He intended to form a new colony on the island.

De Vries returned to Holland and, in Sept 1638, returned to Staaten Eylandt with a group of settlers. The colony prospered for a while, but with continued conflict with the local Indians, they were forced to abandon the settlement.

He left America for the last time in October 1643. In 1655, he wrote a book on the history of Nieuw Netherlands and died in Hoorn, Holland, about 1662.

---

[31] TNA. AO 13. Volume 108. Folio 275/6.

On July 3, 1640, Cornelis Melyn (1600-1662), a Dutch merchant from Antwerp, received a directive from the directors of the Dutch West India Company. In it, they informed him to take possession of Staen Iland, with instructions to "erect it into a colonie."

After some bad fortune, he, his family and about 40 settlers finally arrived in Nieuw Amsterdam on the *Den Eyckenboom* (*Oak Tree*) on Aug 20, 1641.

The Company appointed him patroon of the island, thus giving him all the jurisdiction, power, and preeminence.

The Indians were quite happy to sell land to the new visitors and, in fact, sold Staaten Eylandt three times. In 1636, the Indians sold a part of the island to Michael Pauw, a Dutch West India Company director, and another part to de Vries.

In 1641, the island was sold to Cornells Melyn and in 1670, the last sale was to Governor-General Francis Lovelace (c1621-1675). He was the second English governor of New York. Oloff Stevensen Van Cortlandt was one of the witnesses to the agreement.

The first settlement built in the summer of 1641 on Staaten Eylandt was close to the block fort, which they named Oude Dorp (Old Town). Three times, there were raids by the Indians, when they burnt the town to the ground.

Around 1658, the citizens established a new village two miles west of Oude Dorp. They called the settlement Stony Brook.

After the British took control in 1664, Dutch, French and English settlers populated the island. The Dutch and the French lived happily with each other. But there was often conflict with the English.

The old Dutch colonial government adjudged the island to belong to Nova Caesarea (New Jersey) and within its jurisdiction. They collected the taxes. Some farmers refused to pay their taxes to New Jersey.

Because of this, the Duke of York issued a statement.

"all islands lying in the harbour of New York, which could be circumnavigated in twenty-four hours, should be belong to the Colony of New York, otherwise it should belong to New Jersey".

In 1676, people reported that 100 families were living on the island. But there was neither a church nor a minister.[32]

By 1683, the population had increased to about two hundred families. This figure is exclusive of the two thousand Indians living on the island.

Staten Island's population had risen to about three thousand people when hostilities started. Half of them followed the crown. While the other half supported the patriots.

Stony Brook, the chief settlement on the island, became the county seat in 1683, a position it held until 1729. This changed in 1729 when they transferred the county seat to Cuckoldstown. The village then changed its name to Richmond.

---

[32] Morris's Memorial History of Staten Island. p.94

During the War of Independence, the authorities imposed martial law on the island.

In early July 1776, the British landed a large force of grenadiers and light infantry on Staten Island. General Howe set up his headquarters in the Old Rose and Crown farmhouse between New Dorp Lane and the Black Horse tavern.

Old Rose & Crown farmhouse

Within days, more British reinforcements arrived, and now the encamped troops outnumbered the residents on the island.

The soldiers constructed defences and reassured the population that they had nothing to fear as long as they remained peacefully at home and showed no sympathy for the rebels.

After the battle of Long Island and the capture of New York, the forces on Staten Island were reduced. The British left just enough soldiers to defend the island against attack.

On 9 September 1776, Philip wrote in his memoir:

To prejudice the minds of the ignorant, against the British Army-

many frightful accounts from Nassau Island & Staaten Island were circulated. Importing the cruel unnatural & inhuman treatment to the Inhabitants from the British Troops. sev'ral persons said to have been murdered in cold blood. Plunging bayonets in their bodies & then trampling them under their horses feet. women without distinction taken into the lascivious embraces of Officers & then turned over to the Soldiery. torn from the arms of husbands and parents by Brutal force-these Accts. (however improbable) gained universal credit & tended to raise resentment to the highest frenzy-

Brigadier-General Skinner spent most of the conflict on Staten Island and New York City. He made his headquarters in the Kruzer (Pelton House) home, built by Joseph Rolph in 1722, at 'The Cove', West New Brighton, where his friend, Mrs General Dufié, lived. The house, originally built as a one-room cottage with a garret, was expanded in 1770. The two families had been friends for many years.

During these troubled times, there were many visitors to the house. Including the Duke of Clarence, the future King William IV. Also, the British soldier and spy, Major John André, was a frequent visitor.

From the house, the Brigadier-General planned raids into New Jersey and intelligence gathering.

In a letter, General Nathanael Greene to Major John Clark, on November 5, 1777, said:

"Intelligence is the life of everything in war."

Pelham House about 1914 with the further extension of 1836, a two-story brick extension that was added to the central section.

Wikimedia Commons   Photographer unknown.

****

5 NEW JERSEY VOLUNTEERS

Philip joined the British Army on December 11, 1776, under the command of Sir William Howe and General Cortlandt Skinner. They made him a lieutenant-colonel and then offered him a warrant to raise a New Jersey unit of Loyalists. He was unsuccessful in this.

After a meeting of the command officers on December 11, they appointed Philip as the Second Major of the brigade of the New Jersey Volunteers. He would serve under Brigadier General Cortlandt Skinner. He held this post for eighteen months.

The New Jersey Volunteers were a Loyalist Provincial regiment serving the British Army during the conflict. During the years of fighting, Cortlandt Skinner initially raised six units. They formed the 1st Battalion of the New Jersey Volunteers on July 1, 1776. They were under the command of Lieutenant-Colonel Elisha Lawrence. In late November 1776, under the command of Lieutenant-Colonel John Morris, they formed the 2nd Battalion.

Additionally, in November, Lieutenant-Colonel Edward Vaughan Dongan set up the 3rd battalion. He became their commanding officer. Philip later became the second major in the 3rd Battalion.

Lieutenant-Colonel Abraham Van Buskirk, a former Bergen County surgeon from Teaneck, commanded the 4th Battalion. They commissioned the battalion on November 16, 1776, and quickly formed ten companies of various strengths. Daniel Isaac Brown became the battalion's first major.

The second major was Robert Timpany, with Captains William Van Allen and Samuel Hayden. A further four companies were raised in early 1777.

When they formed the 4th Battalion, few people expected the war would last long, and most soldiers estimated to be home within months. Philip joined the 4th Battalion as a Major on April 25, 1778.

There was also a 5th Battalion formed in November 1776 and a 6th Battalion raised in December 1776. They later merged with other battalions because the army considered them to be under strength.

The British referred to these Loyalist units as the Provincial Corps. They were not part of the British Army, which was controlled by the Home Office. They came under the control of the Inspector General of Provincial Forces and Lieutenant-Colonel Alexander Innes. It was the Treasury Office that arranged supplies of food, clothing, and equipment.

On enlisting, a soldier received two guineas (a guinea is one pound and one shilling) as a bounty, which increased in later years to three guineas. The pay rose to six guineas in 1781. They received the same provisions, pay (sixpence a day for a private), arms and clothing as their British comrades.

The authorities expected the enlisted soldiers to serve anywhere in North America for the duration of the war. At this time, the men did not receive uniforms, so they wore whatever clothing they had at home. They were immediately responsible for duty or combat. Van Buskirk's battalion was sent into action within two weeks of being formed.

It was April 1777 when the British sent the first shipment of uniforms for the Provincial units. This was a green full-length regimental coat with white lapels, white waistcoat, white stockings and white knee breeches. They also supplied black shoes, a cocked hat, muskets, and bayonets. Initially, Cortlandt Skinner's soldiers wore green uniforms and earned the nickname 'Skinner's Greens'.

Every year, the army supplied new uniforms. Sometimes they were green and other times red, just like the regular British army. By 1780, red coats, with blue facings and white lace, were the standard attire.

Officers generally purchased their own uniforms made up to a regimental pattern, with silver lace and epaulettes, a silver laced hat with silver loop and a feather, a red silk sash, silver gorget (a single piece of armour to protect the throat and neck. This was part of the British Army's uniform until 1830 and only used for decoration and not worn on campaigns.) and silver-mounted sword and belt plate.[33]

Clothing & Supplies

State of Cloathing in the Stores of the Inspector General of Provincial Forces at New York. April 25th 1781.[34]

In New York

Serjeants- 276 Coats, 74 Jackets, 407 Waist Coats, 271 Breeches, 51 Sashes.
Drummers- 129 Coats, 35 Jackets, 130 Waist Coats, 125 Breeches, 70 Belts & Slings.
Privates- 6658 Coats, 542 Jackets, 6927 Waistcoats, 5117 Breeches.

1700 Leather Breeches, 9000 Shirts, 5921 Stocks and Buckles, 14986 Shoe pairs, 5236 Stocking pairs, 3416 Buckle pairs, 1128 Boot pairs, 15314 Shoe Soals pairs, 5191 Hats, 3234 Mittens, 20981 Leggings, 143 White Epaulettes, 692 Yellow Epaulettes, 22 Gold Epaulettes.

---

[33] The Online Institute for Advanced Loyalist Studies. Clothing and Supplies. NJV 1776-1783.

[34] Source: State of Cloathing in New York and Charleston, Alex. Innes, 25 April 1781, Clinton Papers Vol. 53, f. 25, Clements Library, online at http://www.royalprovincial.com/military/supp/supstat1.htm accessed 18/106/2024.

Most New Jersey Volunteer units became part of the garrison stationed on Staten Island and Bergen Neck. (Bergen Neck is a peninsula some 3 miles long and lies between Newark and Upper New York bays.)

They conducted raids against rebel homes and fighters in Bergen County. New York City was the major stronghold for Loyalists and the British Army. Its population at this time was 5,000 persons. By the evacuation of 1783 and the influx of Loyalists seeking protection, it rose to 33,000.

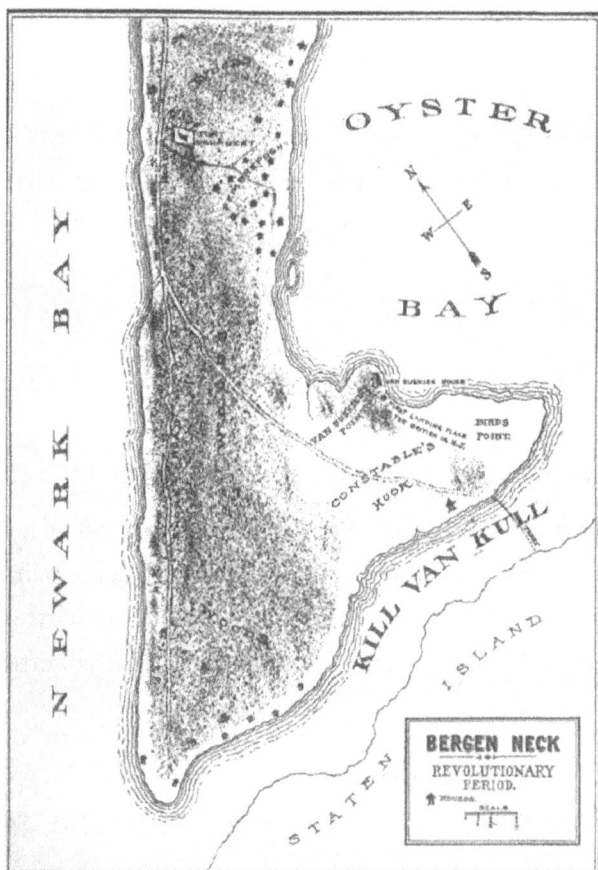

In 1775, there was an outbreak of smallpox, with the disease breaking out in both American and British camps.

From Morristown on February 6, 1777, General Washington wrote to Dr William Shippen Jnr (1736-1808), the third Director General of the Continental Army. The General requested Dr Shippen to start smallpox inoculations of the troops.[35] Later, in February, Washington informed Congress of his plans to mass vaccinate his troops.

On January 20, 1777, Catharine sent Philip another letter recording her problems. The area was full of rebel troops who would stop at their house for food and to tend their horses. Sometimes, soldiers would stay the night. Afterwards, they stationed soldiers in the house.

My beloved Philly[36]

Since my last letter to you a great variety of troubles
and afflictions have beset our dear family and put your
Kitty's resolution to its utmost strength. The arrival of
the Rebel Troops in this neighbourhood has been
severely felt by us. Parties continually passing this way
were always directed by officious people to stop at our
house to breakfast, dine, or stay the night; the horses
from the teams were put into our barns to feed, without
even the ceremony of asking liberty. During the stay of
the officers of the hospital we had some protection. But
immediately on their removal, several field officers from
the New England line and a company of privates took
possession, a number of men were put into the kitchen
and store. They were the most disorderly of their
species and their officers were from the dregs of the
people. Indeed, two lieutenants messed and slept in the

[35] *National Archives*,
https://founders.archives.gov/documents/Washington/03-08-02-0281.
[36] Vernon-Jackson, H. O. H., "A Loyalist's Wife: Letters of Mrs Philip Van Cortlandt December 1776 to February 1777", *History Today Magazine*, Volume XIV, no. 8, Pages 574-580.

kitchen altogether, and would not be prevailed upon to leave their quarters. To complete the whole, a French general has also come on the hill at Dashwood, and daily draws his supply for his numerous cavalry from our granary and barrack.

Many of our female neighbours have been here, but I find their visits are only to gratify curiosity and to add insult to our unremitted distress. One of them who lives across the river, whose family we took so much pleasure in relieving when friendless, made a return of gratitude yesterday by a humane speech. She said that formerly she always respected you and loved the ground over which you walked, but now could with pleasure see your blood run down the road. Her husband came a night or two past, with a number of others, around one o'clock, on pretense to search for a British Light Horseman who they were informed was secreted in our house. On being assured that such a supposition was ridiculous, as the house was guarded day and night, and no one permitted to speak to me but in presence of an officer or the sentry, they then acknowledged their errand was to look for you, as they had positive orders to take you dead or alive and were determined to do it. After much abuse they went off, though not before one of the officers in the house told them you was not at home. The pious, devout and Reverend Mr. Green is very industrious in promoting your ruin by declaring you an enemy to their cause. The farmers are forbid to sell me provisions, and the millers to grind our grain. Our woods are cut down for the use of their army, and that which you bought and left corded near the river my servants are forbid to touch, though we are in the greatest distress for the want of it, as you may suppose when I assure you that our dear

children have been six weeks without any other covering
to their tender feet, but woollen rags sewed round
them to keep them from freezing.

A few days ago, the colonel and other officers quartered here
told me they expected some of their brother officers to
dine and spend the evening with them.

This I understood as a hint to provide
accordingly, which I was determined to do to the
utmost of my powers, *though from necessity*. The dinner
was plentiful, well-dressed, and such as I wished to have
given to more welcome guests. The old Madeira was
drank in profusion; and, if we judge from the eating and
drinking, they paid a compliment to our entertainment.

After removal of the cloth, I took the earliest
opportunity with our dear children to absent myself; and
then they set in for a drinking match, every few minutes
calling aloud upon the *landlady* to replenish the
decanters which were kept continually going. It grieved
me to see the countenances of our little ones. I
endeavoured to conceal my emotions, but did it
awkwardly. At length, one of them observed that the
Gentlemen who used to dine with Pappa never did so;
and, if these were not his friends, why did Mamma treat
them so well. The guests now grew noisy; and, in order
to shun it, I ordered one of the servants to sit in the
back room with the keys and a lantern ready to obey
their calls for wine. I then took our children to the little
Island behind the Garden to beguile the time; and,
whilst they were diverting themselves in picking up
sticks to kindle a fire and cut little fish out of the ice, I
sat down under the beautiful spreading branches of the
lofty Elm which we in Summer season daily visited with
mutual uninterrupted pleasure.

Though the weather was cold, I did not perceive it until my return to the house, which was much sooner than I wished.

A Servant came down and said the Gentlemen desired my company, as they were going to dance.

This confounded me. I hastened with our flock into the back room, where I had not been long before the colonel knocked at the door and being admitted told me, 'the fiddler and the guests were assembled and he hoped I would honour them with my Company.' Though I was much distressed, my resolution supported me whilst I told him that the present situation of myself and children would sufficiently apologize for my refusing to partake of any scenes of mirth where my husband could not attend me. This brought the tears from my eyes, which before had been suppressed, and relieved me from any further importunity until near ten o'clock when he returned and entreated me 'to honour the Company for a few minutes as a Spectator.' I thought it best to make merit of necessity and, taking the older children with me, placed ourselves between the clock and back room door. The Officers were dancing Reels with some tawdry dressed females I had never seen, and among them the colonel's housekeeper, whom I did know. I felt shocked and from the behaviour of the company resolved to withdraw, and [found] strength sufficient to reach my room with our dear children, whose eyes were all swimming in tears, and passed the remainder of the night without further interruption.

Men from the rebel army regularly raided the family home. They stole the family's food supplies and even took the children's clothes.

86

It was necessary for the children, now without shoes, to have rags wrapped around their feet to protect them from the cold. Soldiers treated the house and staff as a common inn.

These were traumatic days for Catharine and the children. The family was very short of food and sometimes went for some days without eating.

Local republicans insisted no one was to sell products to the family or grind grain from the estate. Most of their friends were turning against the family. Even their local minister turned against them, claiming Philip was "an enemy to their cause."

Catharine sent another letter from Hanover on February 12th. She informed Philip that she had at last received his letter from Green Pond Mountain, Sussex. But the rebels had intercepted it. Below is an extract of her letter:

My beloved husband,[37]

On her [servant Phillis'] return from the pump, she heard (as she afterwards declared) the tread of a strange horse's feet. She looked round, put down her pails of water, and went immediately back into the road.

By this time a Man had got opposite the house, who she was certainly convinced was a British Light Horseman.

He asked her master's name, and on being informed, said, *he was right, that you was a Field Officer at New York.*

He then desired her to ask her mistress to direct him to a place of safety as he was a stranger and upon business, and had been recommended to enquire here.

When she delivered the message to me, I could scarcely support myself on account of the risk; for, though the Soldiers were gone who

---

[37] Vernon-Jackson, H. O. H., "A Loyalist's Wife: Letters of Mrs Philip Van Cortlandt December 1776 to February 1777", *History Today Magazine*, Volume XIV, no. 8, Pages 574-580.

had been in the kitchen, another Company had come and taken
possession of the children's nursery, and were gone about a
mile to draw their provisions.

The Officers had rode out to Morristown; still there was a Guard
left behind, which was asleep except for the two sentries, and the one
from the front had moved round the corner of the house to be out of
the wind, which having observed I took courage to describe
a house where he might trust a man who would behave to
him in a particular manner.

Just as he trotted off, the sentry observed him, though too late to
make any other discovery than that a Stranger with a fur cap, brown
great coat, and mounted on a fine black horse with a white face and
four white feet, had stopped and spoke to one of the family.

These mysterious circumstances, joined to the Officers' having
heard that General Washington had intercepted a letter from you to
me, conspired to cause them to be more watchful on
my conduct afterwards.

The letter I allude to was dated 'Green Pond Mountain, Sussex,'
which was taken from a boy near Hanover bridge, who, with the letter,
was carried to Head-quarters at Morristown, where the General
and his Company were just at dinner.

The letter was read aloud, as I was informed by a person who was at
no great distance, and disappointed both zealous patriots as
well as critics.

The boy was dismissed with a shilling, and I got my letter sealed
under a cover.

The narrow escape of your last was something remarkable.

I was sitting about the dusk of evening in my room, very
disconsolate with our dear children around me, reflecting on our
deplorable situation and the gloomy prospects before me, when I heard
a sudden rap at the street door.

Forgetting the servants in the kitchen, I went myself to see who it
was, and lucky I did.

A tall, thin man presented himself, and on my stooping to
unbolt the door whispered, he had a letter for me.
My heart fluttered.
The sentry was walking before the door, and two of the Officers
were coming towards me.
I recollected myself and '*desired the good man to walk into my room
until I could give him a little wine for the sick' woman*.'
He took the hint, and as soon as he came to my fireside gave me a
letter, the outside of which I just looked at and threw it
under the head of my bed and immediately set about getting him
some wine for his wife to prevent suspicion.
He faithfully delivered your verbal answer to my verbal message to
you, which afforded balmy comfort to your afflicted Kitty who now
begins to want support in proportion as her trials grow severe.
The honest man after taking a dram went away, being followed out
of doors and questioned by the Officers, who had been venting,
cursing and swearing against the sentry for permitting anyone to
approach the house or speak to me without their first
being acquainted with it.
On their return to the room, they seemed more composed though I
am convinced from their conduct since that their
suspicions are not removed.
The frequent frolics of the Officers in the house, the Soldiers in the
Nursery, and Cattle constantly fed here has reduced our late Stock
of plenty to a miserable pittance.
The other day was almost too much for me.
We had been several days without bread and were subsisting upon a
half bushel of Indian meal which had been given me by a Dutch farmer
I did not know, who said he had heard of our situation and
would take no pay.
I felt gratitude and thanked the honest Stranger for his present.
Our repast for dinner was a small piece of salt pork with the Indian
meal friend in hog's fat, of which we made a dainty feast.

Our stock of meal had been expended five days and the
Soldiers not being about, our little Sally immediately went
into the Nursery, and picking up a piece of dirty bread
which had been trod under their feet came running up to me,
wiping it with her frock, and with joy sparkling in her
eyes presented it to me crying out, 'Do eat it, Mamma. 'Tis good.
'Tis charming good bread. Indeed, it is. I have tasted it.'
This was too much. I reeled to a chair, and told the child I
was sick and could not eat it.

The next day Doctor Bond (a favourite and one of General
Washington's family) came to a house, and passing me suddenly went
into the back room and taking from under his coat a loaf of bread, he
gave it to the children and before I could thank him he ran past
me with his handkerchief and hat before his face.

My situation was now become unsupportable. I sent to Mr. Joseph
B_____ on the hill, and requested him to accompany me to Morristown.
During our ride he did not say much. He sometime's attempted to
speak, but seemed choked. Indeed, his behaviour ever since my dear
husband's absence has been friendly and more like a brother's
sympathy than a stranger's.

When we came to Sister Makie's, I was introduced to General
Sinclair (who was formerly a British Officer) and told him my request
was to obtain General Washington's protection in writing for myself
and helpless children from further insult from his Army.

He seemed much affected and assured me he would immediately
wait on the General and state my case to him.

After staying in General Washington's quarters about an hour, he
returned and sent into the room for Mrs. Makie and told her (with
tears running down his cheeks) that he could not see me, as he had
represented my situation and request to the General with the fullest
confidence of Success, but had the mortification of a refusal, 'unless
Mr. CORTLANDT would return from the British lines and
on no other condition.'

A few days after, Doctor Bond came here and with a faltering voice
told me he was sent by General Washington to inform me that it was

his positive orders that our house should be taken as an Hospital to
innoculate his Army with the smallpox, and if I chose he would
innoculate my family at the same time.
I thanked him.
He saw my agitation and shed tears, and promised to use his
influence with the General to obtain the only favour I had
now to ask of him; which was, to go to my husband with my
children, servants, and such effects as I could take with me, as I was
now reduced to the lowest distress and did not choose to be
come a burden to Strangers.

Occasionally, some good neighbours smuggled food to Catherine and
the children, and they would decline any payment. In desperation,
Catharine travelled to Morristown to get General Washington's
protection.

The General refused to help the family until Philip came back from
the British lines. He insisted he would not help until Philip returned.
And on no other condition. A few days later, the rebels informed
Catharine that their large riverside manor house, which had housed the
family and staff of servants, was to be used as a hospital for six hundred
soldiers. It was because of the recent outbreak of smallpox spreading
amongst the Colonial troops.

This was during the smallpox epidemic that raged through the
colonies and the Continental Army. The colonies suffered many
outbreaks of the disease during the 1700s. This badly affected the
Americans. Smallpox plagued the Continental Army as well as the
civilian population. The British troops had previously encountered the
disease in Europe and did not suffer many casualties.

The doctors offered to inoculate Catherine and the children.

After Catharine's approach, Dr Nathaniel Bond (1745-1777), a
military surgeon and the doctor in charge, agreed to try to influence
General Washington. He would help the family get a permit.

That would allow Catherine and the family to depart for New York and join Philip. Doctor Bond was a relative of General Washington.

Finally, on February 15th, General Washington agreed to issue a safe passage permit for Catharine and her family so she could join her husband in New York.

On February 19th, Catherine sends another letter advising Philip that General Washington has finally issued a pass for the family to leave. The transcript of her letter vividly describes her journey. It details their horrendous journey and the hostility shown to Loyalist families. It also shows the fondness between her and Philip.

Her fourth and last letter was from Hoebuck (Hoboken) Ferry and dated February 19th, 1777:

My beloved husband,[38]

Doctor Bond succeeded and with orders for my removal brought me General Washington's pass which I now enclose.

To describe the scene at parting with our few though sincere friends, the destruction of our property, the insulting looks and behaviour of those who had been accessory to our ruin, the situation of our beloved children and faithful servants on the day we were turned off from our once peaceful and happy cottage, in a cold snow storm, with my feelings on the occasion, is more than I dare attempt. At four in the afternoon, a cold, disagreeable day, we bid adieu to our home to make room for the sick of General Washington's Army and, after an unpleasant and fatiguing Journey, arrived at twelve o'clock at night at the Fork of the Rivers Rockaway, Pompton and Haakinsack.

A Young Woman, whose father and brother were both in the Rebel service, was much affected with my Situation and endeavoured to remove me into another room.
The next evening, after a most distressing ride through snow and rain with much difficulty in changingg Carriages for, ourselves and baggage, we arrived at Campbell s Tavern at Haakinsack, the mistress of which refused me admittance when she was informed whose family it was alleging

---

[38] Vernon-Jackson, H. O. H., "A Loyalist's Wife: Letters of Mrs Philip Van Cortlandt December 1776 to February 1777", *History Today Magazine*, Volume XIV, no. 8, Pages 574-580.

as an excuse that she expected a number of Officers, and
notwithstanding my earnest entreaties only to permit

me to have shelter in one of her empty rooms for myself and
children from the inclemency of the weather, as I could
make use of my own beds though wet.

The town was filled with Soldiers and the night advancing.
Whilst reflecting on my situation, a person came up to
me, looked me in the face, and asked me to accompany
him to his Uncle's house with my whole family. I did
not thank him, though I attempted more than once; he
read my gratitude in my countenance. On entering a
room with a large fire, it had an effect on the children,
whose stomachs had been empty the greatest part of
the day, that caused instant puking and was near
proving fatal to them.

The next morning early, we again set off in a most
uncomfortable sleet and snow, and rode until ten o
clock, when our youngest children could not pass a
farmyard where they were milking cows without
wishing for some. My little Willing was almost in
agonies, springing in my Arms and calling for milk. I
therefore rode up and requested the good man to let me
have some from one of his pails. He partly advanced.
My dear boy reached out his arms.

The man stopped, asked who we were and, upon being
informed by the driver, swore bitterly he would not give
a drop to any Tory Bitch. I offered him money, my
children screamed; and, as I could not prevail, I drove
on.

On my airrival here, it was necessary for me to take some
repose, after which my anxiety was considerable until the
coming of the servants who had been obliged to leave me
soon after setting off from Haakinsack, on account

of the baggage and the badness of the roads. About

two hours ago, they come in and inform me that crossing

the river on the ice at the ferry, they were stopped and fired upon by a party of armed Rebels, nearly killing several of them (as a ball went through Old Sam's hat). Upon being shewn a copy of General Washington's pass, the original being with me, they damned the General 'for giving the mistress a pass,' ·and said they were sorry they had, not come a little sooner as they would have stopped the whole, but swore they would make a prize of the three loads they had in their possession, and immediately fell to plundering chests, trunks, boxes, etc., throwing the heavy Articles into a hole in the ice, and breaking a barrel of old-fashioned China into a thousand pieces. The Officers of this Party are a Captain Dodd and Lieutenant Irvin. The former put on your new plaid Gown which he wore. The small remains of our property is now here; and, after paying the drivers in hard money and expenses on the road, but little remains. With that little, let us now, my dear Philly, be content, and though fortune frowns we will still be happy, in each other. When we parted a few months ago, I was hearty and blooming; but be not surprised, my dear Pappa, if you see your Kitty altered. Indeed, I am much altered.

But I know your heart, you will not love me less, but heal with redoubled affection and tenderness the wounds received in your behalf for those principles of loyalty which alone induced you to leave to the mercy of Rebels, nine innocent children and your fond and ever

affectionate Wife,

C.V.C."

Details of the pass issued by General Washington to Catherine.[39]

Mrs Catharine Cortlandt, wife of Philip Cortlandt. Esq, now in New York or Long Island and to carry with her, her Servants, Furniture and Apparel,

Given under my Hand at Head Quarters at Morris town this 15th day of February 1777.

G. Washington

At last, Catharine rejoined her husband in New York City. The family returned to Catharine's parental home in Jamaica for a short time.

In October, the family stayed in Augustus Van Cortlandt's house before returning to New York City. Here, they occupied their old house in the city.

On March 23, 1777, Gertrude Beekman (1682-1777), daughter of Stephanus Van Cortlandt and Philip's aunt, died at her home. She was a wealthy woman and left a large plot of land in the manor of Cortlandt to her nephew, Pierre Van Cortlandt.

Gertrude also bequeathed in her will, land to Philip and his brother, William Ricketts. This included some rights to part of the manor of Cortlandt in the land known as South Lot Number 8.

This lot, some 2,394 acres, was by John Peek's Creek near the township of Bedford. A quarter interest in the land known as the Rombout Patent was also bestowed.

In later years, Philip would detail the property he held to the Commissioners in London, inquiring about the losses of the American Loyalists in his claim for compensation.

---

[39] TNA AO 13. Volume 54.

In New York, Catharine gave birth to another son, whom they named Jacob Ogden (1777–27 September 1811).

As a young teenager, in 1782, he joined the Loyal American Regiment as an ensign. After the disbandment of his regiment, he joined the British Army. Jacob became a captain. He died on active service in Europe during the Napoleonic Wars in September 1811.

The Provincial Congress in May 1777 appointed the first Committee of Safety. This was made up of leading citizens who were responsible for creating a temporary government and passing laws until they chose a governor. Philip's uncle, Pierre Van Cortlandt, was first appointed vice-chairman. And then the chairman of the Congress.

Pierre later held the office of Lieutenant-Governor of New York. A position he held from 1777 until 1795. The family at Cortlandt Manor, Westchester County, were staunch colonialists, and Pierre formed a close relationship with George Washington.

In November 1776, November 1779 and between June and July 1781, the manor house served as George Washington's headquarters.

Following intense debates, they approved the Flag resolution at the Continental Congress meeting on June 14th.

Here, they adopted a new flag bearing 13 stars and 13 stripes. This symbolised the newly independent federal republic of the United States of America.

The stars, now five-pointed on a blue background, represented the original 13 colonies (today 50 states). With the horizontal stripes, red and white alternating, denoting the 13 colonies.

The resolution passed said, "the flag of the United States be 13 stripes, alternate red and white", and that "the union be 13 stars, white in a blue field, representing a new constellation."

On June 5, 1777, at the Congress meeting, they offered an unconditional pardon to Loyalists. This was on the condition that they would swear an oath of allegiance to the newly independent Republic of America. If they refused, the state's commissioners would seize and sell their lands and personal property.

Philip receives orders to march from Bergen to Staten Island with the Jersey Brigade, where they were to join up with Lieutenant-Colonel Edward Vaughan Dongan.

On August 22, 1777, the Continental Major General John Sullivan, with Generals De Bourgh and William Smallwood, and 2,000 rebel soldiers invaded Staten Island. This was an unexpected attack. And they caught the 1st and 6th battalions of New Jersey Volunteers by surprise.

In the battle, the patriots captured two officers, Lieutenant-Colonel Elisha Lawrence and Lieutenant-Colonel Joseph Barton, and eighty men.

During Sullivan's raid, Philip's 29-year-old friend Lieutenant-Colonel Edward Dongan, commander of the 3rd Battalion, was injured.

This was at a skirmish that took place between the Old Blazing Star Ferry located about halfway between Elizabeth and Amboy, and Prince's Ba's Bay. On August 24th, in a hospital in New York City, Lieutenant-Colonel Dongan died from his wounds. By coincidence, his young son died the same day. They were buried together in a grave[40] at Trinity Church graveyard, New York.

In the York Gazette and Weekly Mercury on September 1, 1777, they published news of Dongan's death.

Lieutenant-Colonel Dongan's death devastated the battalion, as he was a well-respected officer. Feelings were very strong among his men, and this led to many officers leaving. Ultimately, the authorities disbanded his battalion. High Command amalgamated the remaining soldiers with the 4th battalion.

The Colonial attack proved unsuccessful, leading to the loss of 10 American fighters and the injury of 15–20 others before they retreated. The British captured over 250 republicans, mainly First and Second Maryland Brigade Continental troops. British casualties were about 5 killed, 7 wounded, and 84 missing.

Sir William Howe, in October 1777, issued two proclamations. The first, on October 1st, required anyone who had been aiding the rebellion in Pennsylvania to swear an oath of allegiance to His Majesty.

The other one announced on October 8th that recruits joining the Provincial Troops would receive a grant of land in the colonies after their corps was reduced or disbanded.

In February and March 1778, there was a severe smallpox outbreak that affected the 4th Battalion of the New Jersey Volunteers. Many of the soldiers in the battalion became ill.

---

[40] TNA. AO13. Volume 109. Folio 49-50

By His EXCELLENCY
Sir *WILLIAM HOWE*, K. B.
General and Commander in Chief, &c. &c. &c.

PROCLAMATION.

WHEREAS for the more speedy and effectual suppression of the unnatural rebellion subsisting in North-America, it has been thought proper to levy a number of Provincial Troops, thereby affording to his Majesty's faithful and well-disposed subjects, inhabitants of the colonies, an opportunity to co-operate in relieving themselves from the miseries attendant on anarchy and tyranny, and in restoring the blessings of peace and order with just and lawful government: As a reward for the promptitude and zeal of his Majesty's faithful subjects who may enter into the corps now raising, I DO HEREBY, in consequence of authority to me given by his Majesty, promise and engage, That all persons who have, or do hereafter inlist into any of the said Provincial Corps, to serve for two years, or during the present war in North-America, and shall continue faithfully to serve in any of the said Corps agreeable to such their engagements, shall, after being reduced or disbanded, obtain, according to their respective stations, grants of the following quantities of vacant lands in the colonies wherein their corps have been or shall be raised, or in such colony as his Majesty may think fit.

Every non-commissioned officer, 200 Acres.
Every private soldier, - - 50 ditto.

The same to be granted to such of the said non-commissioned officers and soldiers as shall personally apply for the same, by the Governor of the respective colonies, without fee or reward, subject, at the expiration of ten years, to the same quit-rents as other lands are subject to in the province within which they shall be granted, and subject to the same conditions of cultivation and improvement.

Given under my hand at Head-quarters in Germantown, this 8th Day of Oct. 1777.
W. HOWE.

By his Excellency's command,
ROBERT MACKENZIE, *Secretary.* [41]

---

[41] LLMC-Digital Collection.

The General Hospital[42] in New York City reported that between the 8th & 15th of February 187 soldiers from the 4th Battalion of the New Jersey Volunteers were affected. They estimated that about 40 men died, with others unable to serve. Later, they discharged the affected soldiers from duty.

After the recent battles and disease outbursts, General Skinner decided he wanted to reduce the number of battalions in the New Jersey Volunteers. Only Van Buskirk's battalion had reached the authorised number of 10 companies.

There was another tragedy for the Van Cortlandt family when Richard Willing, Phillip, and Catherine's young son, died on March 16, 1778, and they buried him in Grace Episcopal churchyard in Jamaica, Queens County.

The records show Philip in the list of officers as a second major in the 3rd battalion. But without pay.

On orders from Alexander Innes, the Inspector General of Provincial Forces, and General Skinners' agreement, they recommended that battalion strength should be reduced from ten companies to five.

Because of the reorganisation in April 1778 of the New Jersey Volunteers, the 4th Battalion was reduced from six battalions to four, the 1st and 5th amalgamated as did the 3rd and 6th battalions. Philip was at last receiving pay.

They transferred Philip to the 4th battalion on April 25, 1778, as their new major on Staten Island.[43] Philip acted as Major of the Brigade for 18 months.

---

[42] "Return of Sick and Wounded in his Majesty's Hospital at New York between the 8th & 15th February 1778. Clinton Papers, 31:9, CL

[43] Muster roll of 31 August (Todd Braisted).

On April 18, 1778, the Congress legislature acknowledged the failure of its previous instructions to those disloyal to the new state. They issued lists of accused Loyalists to be tried in each county. A guilty verdict would affect all their properties, regardless of the county in which they were located. Retribution was taking place. The rebels had orders to confiscate Philip's New Jersey property holdings.

Colonial officials confiscated the house contents and Philip and his family's personal belongings and sold them on June 8, 1778, for the derisory sum of £156. 5s 6d in Continental money.

As reported in the New Jersey Gazette, he was about to lose all his other family assets and any right to claim on the Cortlandt Manor, the ancestral family home.

Reported by The New Jersey Gazette (Trenton), December 16, 1778.

> THIS is to give notice, that there has been judgment entered the last court against Thomas MILLIDGE, Stephen SKINNER, Anthony HOLLENHEAD, John TROOP, John STEWARD, Ezekial BEACH, Joseph CONLIFF, Hugh GAINE, John BOYLS, John THORBORN, Asher DUNHAM, William DEAMAN, Philip VAN CORTLAND, Jacob HILOR, Humphrey DAVENPORT, William HOWARD, George BEATTEE, Jacob DEMAREST, Isaac HORNBECK, John BOWLSBY, Edward BOWLSBY, Charles BOWLSBY, Richard BOWLSBY, Thomas HUSK, Lawrence BUSKIRK, Samuel RYERSON, and Nicholas VURLANDT, as the law directs, for their having joined the enemy against their country;
>
> and all persons that have any demands against any of their estates, are desired to meet and make it

appear at the house of Matthias Burnet, Esq. in
Hanover, on the second Wednesday in January next,
at ten o'clock A.M. that it may be settled; and all
persons indebted, are desired to pay the money as
soon as possible, or have any of their effects, to deliver
them up to the Commissioners, or they may depend
upon being dealt with as the law directs.

Alex. Carmichael,   }   Commis-

Aaron Kitchel,   }   sioners.

Morris-County, Dec. 7, 1778.

Many Loyalists reluctantly submitted to swear the oath. As they
wished to keep their lands and property.

Samuel Cooke, an Anglican minister from Shrewsbury, wrote,
"Those who remain behind conform no farther to the present Tyranny
than is absolutely necessary for their safety, and to exempt them from
Banishment and Confiscation or Jail."

There was a strong warning to all loyalists when, on February 17,
1779, an advertisement appeared in a New Jersey newspaper. The
advertisement contained the names of seventeen people, and it
advertised the sale of land.

"WHEREAS inquisition has been found, and final County,
judgment entered in favour of the State, against {17 people named} —
Notice is hereby given, that the houses and lands, and leases for life,
and all the real estate that did belong to any or all of them, will be sold
at public venue on Tuesday the 30th day of March next, at the house of
Capt. Jacob Arnold, in Morris-Town, to begin at 10 of the clock, A.
M., on said day, and to continue from day to day by adjournments, till
the whole are sold; and as some of the lands are

not yet surveyed, they cannot be so particularly described, but there will be the draughts shewn on the day of sale, and if there should be any persons from a distance inclining to purchase, and are unacquainted with the premises, by applying to one of the Commissioners they will be shewn, or informed, and deeds will be made out as soon as possible after the sales are over, as the act of the Assembly directs, and the purchasers must pay the money at the signing of the deeds, for the use of this State."

Failing to support the rebel cause had dire effects for Loyalists' families.

The war was continuing, and the number of deserters from their forces was a significant concern for the British as it was for the Republican forces. So, on February 23rd, Sir Henry Clinton (1730–1795), the Commander-in-Chief of His Majesty's forces, issued a declaration. In it, he promised that any man returning to take up arms on behalf of the British would receive a full pardon.

In February 1779, Brigadier-General Cortlandt Skinner, Philip, and William Luce contacted Ephraim Marsh Jnr. They offered him 2,000 guineas and a pension if he would deliver Governor Livingston, the first governor of New Jersey, dead or alive, to them on Staten Island. Marsh refused.

Later in February, the 4th Battalion, under Lieutenant-Colonel Abraham Van Buskirk, with Philip and comprising 250 rank-and-file men and two iron 4 Pounder Cannons, moved from the north end of Staten Island. Where they had been stationed. They were establishing a new outpost at Hoebuck, modern Hoboken, New Jersey[44]. They moved to William Bayard's mansion and estate at Castle Point, Hoebuck.

---

[44] "Return of the Strength and Distribution of His Majesty's Provincial Forces, February 1779." Dreer Collection, Misc. Mss. No. 12, Historical Society of Pennsylvania

He later reported, "his new House and Barn was turned into a place of defence for His Majesty's Service."[45] From here, they could launch raids into Bergen County.

The battalion was regularly engaged in skirmishes against the Bergen County Militia and the 1st and 2nd North Carolina Regiments, who were barracked at Paramus.

On March 2nd, General Maxwell of the Continental Army informs George Washington of the latest movements of the New Jersey Volunteers.[46]

Food shortage was a continuing problem, with the many people sheltering under British protection. Hence, feeding the expanding populations of Long Island and Staten Island became a priority for the occupying forces. General Commander Sir Henry Clinton issued an order in March. He agreed to permit loyal subjects to cultivate any free portion of cleared lands for themselves and their families. He also warned that anyone caught stealing food or cattle or causing harm would face severe action.

Later in the summer, in July, Lieutenant-Colonel Van Buskirk, who had previously been the Bergen County surgeon and Philip's commanding officer, moved the battalion to the garrison at Paulus Hook, now Jersey City. The town was the British Army's permanent base in Bergen County.

Philip's son, Philip Jnr, a young teenager, in July 1779, joined the British army as an ensign with his father's 4th Battalion of the New Jersey Volunteers. He stayed with this unit until the end of the fighting in 1783.

---

[45] TNA. AO12. Volume 12. Folio 60-69.

[46] Library of Congress, George Washington Papers, Series 4, General Correspondence, 10 February 1779–24 March 1779.

The New Jersey Volunteers left Paulus Hook on orders received on October 14th, and moved to Governor's Island, situated in the middle of New York Harbour.

The British high command ordered them to move because they feared a French attack on New York City. They reported that the French fleet was manoeuvring off the American coast.

When the British realised the French would not attack New York, the 4th battalion relocated back to their old barracks at Decker's Ferry, Staten Island, arriving there by December 14th. The battalion stayed on Staten Island for the next two and a half years.

The war was progressing in the Southern Campaign of 1779, and two of DeLancey's battalions were sent to assist. They fought at the siege of Fort Ninety-Six, South Carolina. When the Patriot General Nathan Greene and 1,500 soldiers besieged and attacked the fort.

The New Jersey Volunteers suffered significant losses in the Southern Campaign. Philip was not involved in the excursion to the southern states as the 3rd Battalion stayed in New York City. They were to defend the hamlet of Setauket and Fort Franklin residents from rebel raiding attacks.

After the death of his aunt, Gertruyd Beekman (daughter of Stephanus), Philip and his brother William Ricketts inherited some land and rights on the Cortlandt estate. The land area, known as South Lot No. 8, was currently in the possession of William Jewell and others, according to the records.

On Tuesday, March 30, 1779, and at Jacob Arnold's house, Alexander Carmichael and Aaron Kitchel, as commissioners, advertised Loyalists' lands for sale. On March 31st, they sold Philip's real estate in Hanover for 3,293 1s 6d.[47] in Continental money. This action was just before New York State passed the Act of Attainder or Confiscation Act of October 22, 1779.

---

[47] TNA. AO 13. Volume 83.

In October 1779, while in Jamaica, New York City, Philip contacted Major John André.[48] (1750-1789).

He was the spymaster and the head of British intelligence gathering. And a close friend of General Sir Henry Clinton.

Phillip had received news about a coal mine recently discovered near New York City. The mine was on Patriots' land. Philip wanted the British army major, John André, to support him with His Excellency the Commander-in-Chief, in the mine's approbation.

Major John André was the Adjutant General to Sir Henry Clinton, a position he took up after his regiment returned to England in 1779.

André's father, Antoine (Anthony), was Swiss, and his mother, Marie-Louise, was of French descent. He was born in London on May 2, 1750, and baptised on May 16th at St Martin Orgar church in London. The French Huguenots regularly used the church near Cannon Street.

John was educated in Geneva, Switzerland, and England, and was proficient in French, German, and Italian. He was also a gifted writer, a poet and enjoyed drawing. Before joining the British Army in 1771, he worked for his father, a merchant in London.

Major André travelled to America and visited Philadelphia, where he met and befriended many colonists. He then moved to Canada to join his regiment and became Aide-de-camp to Sir Charles Grey.

Major André, on June 7, 1777, while sharing accommodations with Colonel Simcoe, a close friend, and living in the old Cuckles Towne Inn on Staten Island, wrote his last will and testament, leaving his estate to his family.

André was an ambitious man interested in intrigue. In 1779, he began a secret correspondence with General Benedict Arnold (1741-1801).

He became involved with General Arnold in a plan for the British to capture West Point.

[48] University of Michigan, William L. Clements Library, Sir Henry Clinton Papers, Volume 73, item 10.

The fort, strategically situated on high ground overlooking the Hudson River and 50 miles (ca. 80 km) north of New York. It was prized by both the British and Americans.

Before setting off to see General Arnold, he spent his last night with friends, wining and dining at the Beekman Mansion in New York.

Major John André

Unfortunately for André, whilst trying to return to the British lines on September 23, 1780, seven American militias on patrol half a mile north of Tarrytown discovered him. They found some incriminating documents which were hidden on him and took him prisoner.

André was riding along the road when the men stopped him. He mistook the men as Loyalists, told them he was a British officer, and offered his gold watch to them if they would let him continue.

The men told him they were Americans and detained him after they had searched him.

André had secreted some documents in his boots, and the militiamen found them. They then escorted their prisoner to the nearby American camp commanded by Col Jameson.[49] André was not in his military uniform and was later tried as a spy.

Even though General Washington requested leniency, they hanged André at Tappan, New York, at noon on October 2, 1780, and buried his body at the foot of the gallows.

Major André was respected and well thought of by the British and his American captors. Robert Adam designed a fine monument that they erected in Westminster Abbey, London. The sculptor was Peter Mathias Van Gelder. King George III paid for the memorial that was erected in 1782.

On 10 August 1821, at the request of the Duke of York, André's body was exhumed and brought back to England. On 28 November, they reburied his body in the Heroes' Corner of Westminster Abbey, London.

A century after his death, the Americans erected a memorial in Tappan, Rockland County.

After Major André's death, Major Oliver DeLancey took charge of intelligence for Sir Henry Clinton.

The British occupied the village of Jamaica in Queens County during the whole time of the conflict. They billeted their soldiers here, especially during the winter when major hostilities usually ceased.

---

[49] The Ulster Sentinel, Kingston, New York. 20 June 1827.

On the north side of the settlement, on the side of a hill, were rows of huts to the east and west.

These extended for a mile or more, with streets in between. The huts were partly sunk into the ground and covered with thatch or reeds.

They placed wood boards inside for flooring, and there was a stone fireplace and a chimney of sticks and mortar.

Soldiers held parades between the gathering of huts and the village. Local Justices or other trusted residents housed the officers in the village.

Jamaica had for many years been a popular gathering place for horse racing, with the most favourite tracks being around the course at Beaver Pond. It was an area Philip knew well, as he had once owned a farm in this locale. On October 16th, there was a contest of three heats, racing twice around the course, for a prize of twenty guineas.

The Northeast US experienced one of its harshest winters on record following the worst recorded Caribbean hurricane in 1779-1780. There are reports that the hurricane of October 10, 1780, had winds of over 200 mph (ca. 322 km/h) and killed over 22,000 people. It also sank over 50 French and British warships.

General Washington's troops marched into Pompton (now Riverdale), New Jersey, to set up their winter encampment in the winter of 1779-1780. There was already snow on the ground, some two feet deep. They had previously encamped in the town in the winter of 1776-1777. But this year was to turn out to be very trying for the colonial soldiers.

On the mainland, they recorded the winter as the coldest in the 18th century, and from about November 10th and almost every day until the middle of March, it snowed. Although the winter of 1777-1778 was very severe, the opinion was that this winter was far more destructive, with heavier frosts and snowstorms. In December 1779, the New York Gazette reported[50] –

---

[50] 26 December 1779, New York Gazette.

"The intense cold weather has, within these two days, occasioned the quick-silver in the weather glass to fall four degrees lower than has been observed for the last seven years: several ships. &.. and many lives have been lost by the monstrous bodies of ice floating in our Bay."

Dr. James Thacher, a Continental Army military surgeon, wrote[51]

"January 1st, 1780 – A new year commences, but brings no relief to the sufferings and privations of our army. Our canvas covering affords but a miserable security from storms of rain and snow, and a great scarcity of provisions still prevails, and its effects are felt even at headquarters…."

There was a tremendous snowstorm on January 3, 1780, that lasted for four days and left four to six feet of snow on the ground. The snowstorm destroyed the soldiers' tents and devastated the encampment. Many died, if not from the cold, then from a lack of supplies and food.

Dr. Thacher wrote:

"The weather for several days has been remarkably cold and stormy. On the 3rd instant, we experienced one of the most tremendous snow-storms ever remembered; no man could endure its violence many minutes without danger of his life. Several marquees were torn asunder and blown down over the officers' heads in the night, and some of the soldiers were actually covered while in their tents, and buried like sheep under the snow."

---

[51] James Thacher, Military Journal of the American Revolution…Hartford 1862, p.180-91.

General Washington, in correspondence, noted that soldiers went 'Five or Six days together without bread, at other times as many days without meat, and once or twice two or three days without either."

The waters of the Hudson River (which had not frozen over since the dreadful winter of 1720) and New York Bay were solid.

This made Staten Island and Manhattan part of the mainland.[52] But this did not stop regular incursions and raids by both the Americans and the British.

On January 14th, Major General Lord Stirling (1725-1783), with over 2,700 Continental troops, crossed over the ice from Elizabeth Town to Staten Island, hoping to surprise the British[53]. With the freezing cold and snow on the ground, soldiers suffering from frostbite and many deserters, the attack was a failure.

The severe winter froze over all the saltwater inlets, harbours, and sounds of the Atlantic coastal plain from North Carolina north-eastward. This hampered operations as they remained closed to navigation for a month or more.

They reported that the ice in some parts of New York harbour was eight feet thick, and they had to use ox-drawn sleighs to resupply Staten Island. It was not until February 20, 1780, that the frost abated and the waters around New York became navigable again.

George Washington sent a letter to the Marquis de Lafayette on March 18, 1780, in which he mentioned the severe weather.[54]

> "The oldest people now living in the Country do
> not remember so hard a winter as the one we are now
> emerging from. In a word the severity of the frost

---

[52] 7 February 1780, Rivington's Gazette.

[53] Washington to Stirling, 12 January 1780. George Washington Papers, Series 4, General Correspondence, 23 December 1779-17 March 1780, LOC.

[54] *The Papers of George Washington*, Revolutionary War Series, vol. 25, *10 March-12 May 1780*, ed. William M. Ferraro. Charlottesville: University of Virginia Press, 2017, pp. 82-84.

exceeded anything of the kind that had ever been
experienced in this climate before."

The Continental Army suffered from shortages of food, blankets and
winter clothing. They continued with raids across the British lines,
looking for supplies.

On the evening of January 25, 1780, in response to a raid on the 14th
by American forces led by Brigadier General William Alexander and
Major-General Stirling, the British advanced. The 1st and 3rd Battalions
of the New Jersey Volunteers crossed from Staten Island. They were
under the command of Lieutenant-Colonel Abraham Van Buskirk.

The New Jersey Volunteer Force consisted of one hundred and
thirty-two men.[55] They had an additional twelve British dragoon units
with them. Philip took an active role in a skirmish at Elizabeth Town
Bridge and was wounded[56] during the fighting. His company was
defending the bridge, and during the action, they captured one
American field officer and three privates.

Elizabethtown was the largest town in New Jersey. It stood by the
Elizabeth River, and just across Newark Bay from Staten Island and
south of Newark. During this raid, the British demolished the
Courthouse and the schoolhouse. They also burned down the
Presbyterian Church.

They said they destroyed the church as the Rev. James Caldwell was
its pastor and well-known for his incendiary anti-British sermons.[57]

The war may be continuing, but in Jamaica, Long Island, in 1780,
Catharine gave birth to another boy named Henry Clinton (1780–1864),
their fifth son.

[55] NJA 2.iv, pp 151-2
[56] Cornwallis Papers, TNA. PRO 30. 11/2, folio 19.
[57] NJA2, iv,166.

Like his father, he joined the British Army in adulthood and rose to the rank of lieutenant-colonel of the 31ˢᵗ Foot Regiment, serving in India.[58]

Reports show Henry married a local Indian woman. Although there is no record of her name.

After leaving the army, Henry returned to England. Henry Clinton died at his home in Kensington, London, in 1863. [59]

He had a son who also served in India, who reached a high rank while serving with Maharaja Ranjit Singh (December 1780-1839) in both the Sikh and the British armies.

After a grim winter and with villages crowded with soldiers, sailors, refugees and displaced people, there was much discontent.[60] This was mainly a farming area and had been a British army garrison since the autumn of 1776.

As recorded in historical documents, there were often disputes between residents and soldiers, with residents' private homes in Jamaica and Flushing on Long Island, New York, experiencing numerous invasions during March and April 1780.

These were desperate times, and armed men, some of whom were soldiers, would enter houses and rob the occupants. An example was in May when Dr Jacob Ogden, Philip's father-in-law, filed a complaint against a lieutenant. Dr Ogden claimed the lieutenant insulted and manhandled him.

The army took the matter seriously, and his superiors ordered the lieutenant to apologise for his actions or face further action.

---

[58] National Archives of India, PR_000002356394 General Orders.
[59] General Register Office. England and Wales Civil Registration Indexes. London, England.
[60] JAR 4 March 2019 Don N Hagist.

A few months later, the Rivington Gazette recorded that Dr Ogden died on September 3rd after 'a very painful illness'.

Dr Ogden was born in Newark, New Jersey, in 1721 and moved and practised in Jamaica, Long Island. He was the warden of Grace Church from 1761 until 1780. The doctor wrote several medical dissertations and promoted the use of vaccinations. They interred his body in the Grace Episcopal Churchyard, Jamaica, Queens County, New York, on 5 September 1780.

In the autumn of 1780, significant changes took place within the New Jersey Volunteers' battalions. Following orders from headquarters, each battalion received orders to form a Light Company. Later, they designated the new unit the Provincial Light Infantry.

Circular

Head Quarters New York the 15th August
1780

Sir

His Excellency the Commander in Chief proposes that every provincial Battalion should form a Light Company and has directed me to request that you will immediately appoint such Officers as you conceive best Qualified for that Service, who are then to be permitted to select such Men from the Corps as they think best Calculated for the purpose.
I have the honour to be Sir
Your most obedient
humble Servant
John André Dy. Adt. Gl.

Col: B: Robinson
American Loyalists

Copies of the above was sent to

Colonel Ludlow 3rd DeLancey's
Colonel Fanning K: A: Regimt.
Lieut. Coll. Barton 1st Skinners
Major Colden   2nd   do

Lieut. Coll. Buskirk 4th   do[61]

Because of the changes, Philip moved back to the 3rd battalion under the command of Lieutenant Colonel Isaac Allen.

Records show that in December 1780, Philip was in the 4th Battalion of New Jersey Volunteers.

Returns in December show Philip's corps had the strength of 1 major, 1 lieutenant, 1 ensign, 3 sergeants, 3 corporals, 1 drummer, and 22 privates. By February 1781, they stationed Philip on Long Island with the 3rd battalion.[62]

There were more changes to the battalions when, on July 24, 1781, the 4th Battalion was re-designated as the 'new' 3rd Battalion commanded by Lt. Col. Abraham Van Buskirk, which Philip joined as their major.

He was paid 15/- per day, and his son, Philip Jnr, an ensign, received 3/8d. They renamed the old 3rd Battalion as the 2nd Battalion.

The last major land battle of the American Revolution took place in Yorktown, Virginia. Where General George Washington beat the British commander, General Lord Charles Cornwallis (1738-1805).

The battle began on September 28, 1781, and finally ended on the morning of October 19th. Outnumbered by the Continental Army and their French allies, the British surrendered to the American forces. Estimated casualties of the engagement were America 389, with 88 killed and 301 wounded. The British casualties were 8,589. With 142 killed, 326 wounded and 7,416 missing or captured.

After the American victory, peace negotiations began in March 1782, ending the war and bringing about America's independence.

Because of the heavy casualties incurred in the southern states, the 1st and 2nd Battalions were combined into a renewed 1st Battalion in 1782.

---

[61] Clinton Papers, Volume 275, John André Letterbook, CL.
[62] Library and Archives Canada, RG 8, "C" Series, Volume 1859, Page 49.

The 3rd became the new 2nd Battalion under the command of Colonel Gabriel George Ludlow (1736-1808).

Colonel Ludlow, after evacuating from New York, at the end of the conflict, travelled to England and in September 1784 to Saint John, New Brunswick. In 1785, he became their first mayor.

Catharine's last child born in America was Charlotte (1782–1847). She was later in April 1841 to marry General Sir John Fraser.

Muster rolls of 18 May 1782 report Philip sick in New York, and by 1783, the muster rolls on 4 March show Philip in New Town, Long Island.

In May 1782, Brigadier-General Cortlandt Skinner and Major Philip van Cortlandt supported a claim for compensation from Mr Isaac Post to the commissioners appointed by the Act of Parliament. It was for his son, Sgt Abraham Post of the 3rd Battalion New Jersey Volunteers, who died in action on August 19, 1778, at Paulus Hook. The Republicans had forced Abraham to abandon his property as he was a Loyalist.

Staaten Island 28th May 1782. [63]

I certify that Isaac Post, the bearer hereof, an inhabitant of
New Jersey, Bergen County, came lately in being
obliged to abandon his property, or undergo a
rigorous imprisont. he has ever been a firm loyalist,
and his only son a Serjant in the 3rd Battn., as the
old man has been ever Steady
I recommend him as an object of favor

Cortd: Skinner   B: Gl. &c.

---

[63] TNA. Headquarters Papers of the British Army in America. PRO30/55/41/79.

118

Thomas Murray, Aide-de-camp, New York, on July 9, 1782, confirmed the details of the claim. The Commissioners granted a small allowance.

The British army used to rent premises in town for military use, and there is a copy of a bill dated December.[64]

It was from 1 June to 3 August 1782, confirming a payment to Philip. This was for the rent and use of a store on John Street used by the 3rd New Jersey Volunteers.

In January 1783, Philip sent a letter to Sir Guy Carleton requesting him to continue his privilege of fuel and provisions, as he had a family to support.[65]

With the prospect of the end of hostilities, commanding officers of the New York Provincial units requested support from Sir Guy Carleton.

They presented detailed proposals of their plan on March 14, 1783:[66]

THAT the Offer of Independence to the American Colonies by Great Britain, and the Probability that the present Contest will terminate in the Separation of the two Countries, has filled the Minds of His Majesty's Provincial Troops with the most alarming Apprehensions.

THAT from the purest Principles of Loyalty, and Attachment to the British Government, they took Arms in His Majesty's Service; and relying on the Justice of their Cause, and the Support of their Sovereign and the British Nation, they have persevered with unabated Zeal through all the Vicissitudes of a calamitous and unfortunate War.

---

[64] TNA. Headquarters Papers of the British Army in America.PRO 30/55/58/133
[65] Carlton Papers 6794.20 V85, M-369.
[66] TNA PRO 30. Volume 55. Folio 10072.

THAT their Hearts still glow with Loyalty to their Sovereign, and the same enthusiastic Attachment to the British Constitution which first stimulated them to Action; and nothing can ever wean their Affections from that Government under which we enjoyed so much Happiness.

THAT their Detestation to that Republican System, which the Leaders of the Rebellion are aiming to establish, the fatal Effects of which are already felt, is unconquerable.

THAT whatever Stipulations may be made at a Peace, for the Restoration of the Property of the Loyalists, and Permission for them to return home; yet, should the American Provinces be

seperated from the British Empire, it will be utterly impossible

or those who have served His Majesty in Arms in this

War to remain in the Country. The personal Animosities that arose from civil Dissentions have been so heightened by the Blood that has been shed in the Contest, that the Parties can never be reconciled.

THAT the Officers of His Majesty's provincial Forces have sacrificed not only their Property, but many of them very lucrative Professions, and all their Expectations from their Rank and Connections in Civil Society.

THAT Numbers of them entered very young into the King's Service, and have grown up in the Army; and having no other Profession, and no Family Expectations, or Homes to go to, their Friends being all involved in the common Ruin, they look forward to the Day of their being disbanded with extreme Solicitude.

THAT many of them have Wives, who, born to the fairest Expectations, and tenderly brought up, have been unaccustomed to want; and Children about them, for whose Education and future happiness they feel the most anxious Concern.

THAT many who have served his Majesty in His Provincial Troops, in subordinate Capacities during this War, have been respectable Yeomen, of good Connections, and possessed of considerable Property, which, from Principles of Loyalty and a Sense of Duty, they quitted; and in the Course of this Contest have shewn a Degree of Patience, Fortitude, and Bravery almost without Example.

THAT there are still remaining in the Provincial Line a great Number of Men, who, from Wounds, and from Disorders contracted in Service, are rendered totally unable to provide for their future Subsistence; they therefore look up to that Government in whose Service they have suffered, with all the Anxiety of Men who have no other Hope left. Many of them have helpless Families who have seen better Days.

THAT the Widows and Orphans of the Provincial Officers and Soldiers who have lost their Lives in the King's Service, are many of them reduced to extreme Poverty and Distress, and have no Prospect of Relief but from the Justice and Humanity of the British Government.

These, SIR, are the Difficulties and the Apprehensions under which
His Majesty's Provincial
Troops now labour; and to Your Excellency they look
up for Assistance.

Relying on the gracious Promise of their Sovereign to support and
protect them, and placing the fullest Confidence in Your Excellency's
benevolent
Interposition, and favorable Representations of their
faithful Services, they are induced to ask:

THAT Grants of Land may be made to them in some of His
Majesty's American Provinces, and that they may be assisted in making
Settlements, in order
that they and their Children may enjoy the Benefits
of the British Government.

THAT some permanent Provision may be made for such of the
Non-Commissioned Officers and Private Soldiers as have been
disabled from Wounds, and from Disorders contracted in His
Majesty's Service; and for the Widows and Orphans of the
deceased Officers and Soldiers.

THAT as a Reward for their faithful Services, the
Rank of the Officers may be permanent in America; and
that they all may be entitled to Half-Pay upon the
Reduction of their Regiments.

86 .THIRD NEW-JERSEY VOLUNTEERS.

Rank.	Name.	Regiment.		Army.		
Lt. Col. Com.	Abr. V. Bufkirk,	Nov.	16 1776			
Major,	P. Van Cortlandt,	Dec.	11 76			
CAPTAINS.						
	William Van Allen,	Nov.	23	76		
	Samuel Ryerfon,	March 25		77		
	Jacob Van Bufkirk,	May	13	80		
	Edward Earle,	July	3	81	Nov.	22 1776
	Waldron Blaau,	July	24	81	Nov.	23 76
	Norman M'Leod,	ditto,			Jan.	20 78
	Donald Campbell,	ditto,				
LIEUTENANTS.						
	John Van Bufkirk,	Dec.	7	76		
	James Servanier,	Jan.	2	77		
	John Haflop,	March 15		77		
	John Simmonfon,	Aug	25	81		
	William Stevenfon,	July	24	81	Dec.	22 76
	Jofiah Parker,	ditto,			Dec.	23 76
	George Lambert,	ditto,			Jan.	1 76
	Juftis Earle,	Dec.	18	81		
	Richard Cooper,	Oct.	25	82		
ENSIGNS.						
	Philip Cortlandt, jun.	July	31	79		
	William Sorrel,	ditto,				
	John Jewet,	ditto,				
	Uriah Blaau,	July	24	81	Jan.	13 77
	Henry Van Allen,	Dec.	18	81		
	Robert Woodward,	Dec.	19	81		
	Stephen Ryder,	Dec.	20	81		
	—— Hendorff,	Feb.	5	82		
	Malcolm Wilmott,	Oct.	25	82		
	Chaplain, Daniel Rothwell,	Oct.	25	78		
	Adjutant, John Haflop,	June	1	81		
	Quarter-Mafter, William Sorrel,	Dec.	24	76		
	Surgeon, John Hammell,	Nov.	25	76		

1783 Muster Roll. TNA AO13/69

The officers concerned about land grants in Nova Scotia submitted a second request on 15 March:

THAT in their opinion Three hundred acres of good Land will be sufficient for each Private Soldier, Three hundred and fifty for each Corporal, and Four hundred acres for each Serjeant, with the same allowance to Commission and Staff-Officers as was granted by His Majesty to the Officers of His Troops who served in North-America in the Last War, and were at the conclusion of it reduced to Half-Pay.

THAT the non-commission Officers and Private-Soldiers, be allowed Provisions, Pay, and Clothing for three years, from the time of their taking possession of their Lands.

THAT they be furnished with Arms and Ammunition for the defence of the Settlement, and a proportion of Ammunition for Hunting.

THAT the Setlers be allowed a proportion of Farming Utencils, with Tools, and Materials for Building and for Erecting Mills. [67]

Their plans were very ambitious and far exceeded the British government's. The government plans that were eventually approved did not amount to 350 acres per soldier. Each private soldier and civilian adult male would receive 100 acres, with an additional 50 acres for every family member. Non-commissioned officers would receive an allocation of 200 acres.

In comparison, the allocation to commissioned officers would be 500 to over 1,000 acres of land in proportion. There was a proviso that grantees would have to become settlers and cultivate the land.

---

[67] TNA PRO 30. Volume 55. Folio 741.

On April 8, 1783, headquarters advised the troops that the British government had reached a preliminary peace deal with the Americans.

They had signed the Peace Treaty between England and the 13 states in September. Britain agreed to recognise American independence.

Sir Guy Carleton, the British commander-in-chief, oversaw the evacuation of the Loyalist refugees from New York. The first fleet departed in December 1782. In 1783, there were departures in May through to October, with the last sailing on November 30th. Reports state that 30,000 troops and 40,000 loyal Americans departed New York in 1783. Some of the ships involved in the evacuation were the *Mary*, the *Commerce*, the *Ranger, and* the *Esther*.

Peace at last, and soldiers of the 3rd battalion New Jersey Volunteers boarded the *Esther* bound for Saint John River Valley, Nova Scotia. Over 400 officers, women, and children with servants were on board, all looking forward to a new and peaceful life. By November, the last British troops had left New York. The British Commissary-General in New York, Brook Watson, reported that over 30,000 men, women, and children set sail to different ports across the Empire. Because of the war, many thousands of Loyalists left their homeland. Those escaping used various ports besides New York. Some travelled from Savannah and Charleston. While others journeyed from East Florida to the Bahamas. Quebec was a favoured destination. According to records, 56,000 Loyalists made the journey to Nova Scotia. Not all of these stayed in Nova Scotia, but moved on to make their homes in other countries.

Philip stayed behind to settle his affairs before he and Catharine and their ten children left for Nova Scotia and England. This journey of some 3,000 nautical miles with favourable weather would take about twelve days to arrive in England.

On May 22, 1783, Philip signed a petition for compensation for Elizabeth Marsh. The details of which are in the Carleton papers at Kew as well as in Canada. [68]

---

[68] Page10108 (1) IDCodeV85 Reel M-3.

The last Muster Roll of Major Philip Van Cortlandt's Company, the 3rd Battalion New Jersey Volunteers, was at Camp New Town Creek on August 22, 1783.[69] It showed Philip as their major.

His son was serving in Captain Edward Earle's company on Long Island on August 22nd. Philip has served for seven years in the military, and his son, Philip Jnr, has served for four. On October 10, 1783, the corps disbanded along the River Saint John in what is now New Brunswick, Canada.

A new journey for Philip and his family was about to begin. They had lost their lands and property and would have to start a new life in England. Philip had a large family to support and would need help from friends who had established their lives in England.

The army put Philip on half pay after the British parliament voted for this, and he was to receive a grant of free land.

At this time in the British army, it was usual for officers who could not find a posting to receive half pay, and they would post their names on an inactive list. As a major, Philip initially received £120 p.a. and his sons £60 each as ensigns.

Parliament had recently voted that officers would receive half pay and all ranks would receive free land grants. NCOs and other ranks did not receive any payments. Officers who had retired received half pay. This they received for the rest of their lives, even if their regiments had been disbanded.

Half Pay, as defined in William Duane's military dictionary of 1810, is — a compensation or retaining fee which is paid to officers who have retired from the service, through age, inability &c., or who have been placed upon that list in consequence of a general reduction of the forces, or a partial drafting &c. of the particular Corps to which they belonged.[70]

---

[69] RG 8, "C" Series, Volume 1857, Page 94+97, LAC.
[70] William Duane, A Military Dictionary; Or Explanation of the Several Systems of Discipline of Different Kinds of

Philip and his son were never involved in major battles, and there are few records of their military service.

The battalions of New Jersey Volunteers, to which Philip was attached, were primarily responsible for conducting intelligence gathering. As well as lightning strikes and reconnaissance against the rebels. They also regularly raided surrounding farms for supplies for the British in New York.

The new U.S. Congress agreed on November 3, 1783, to disband the Continental Army. Below is part of the declaration.

"And it is our will and pleasure, that such part of the federal armies as stands engaged to serve during the war, and as by our Acts of the 26 day of May, the 11 day of June, the 9 day August, and the 26 day of September last, were furloughed, shall, from and after the third day of November next, be absolutely discharged by virtue of this our proclamation, from the said service:"[71]

General Washington, with his troops and Governor Clinton on November 22, 1783, entered New York City and so ended British occupation.

Researchers estimate that over 60,000 refugees left America. That figure includes about 10,000 freed slaves. The majority went to New Brunswick and Nova Scotia, with 13,000 travelling to England.

Not all Loyalists left America. Around 500,000 stayed and moved back to their old homes. Keeping their political opinions to themselves.

Troops, Infantry, Artillery and Cavalry; the Principles of Fortification, and All the Modern Improvements in the Science of Tactics, (London, 1810), p.516.

[71] Journals of the Continental Congress --Saturday, October 18, 1783.

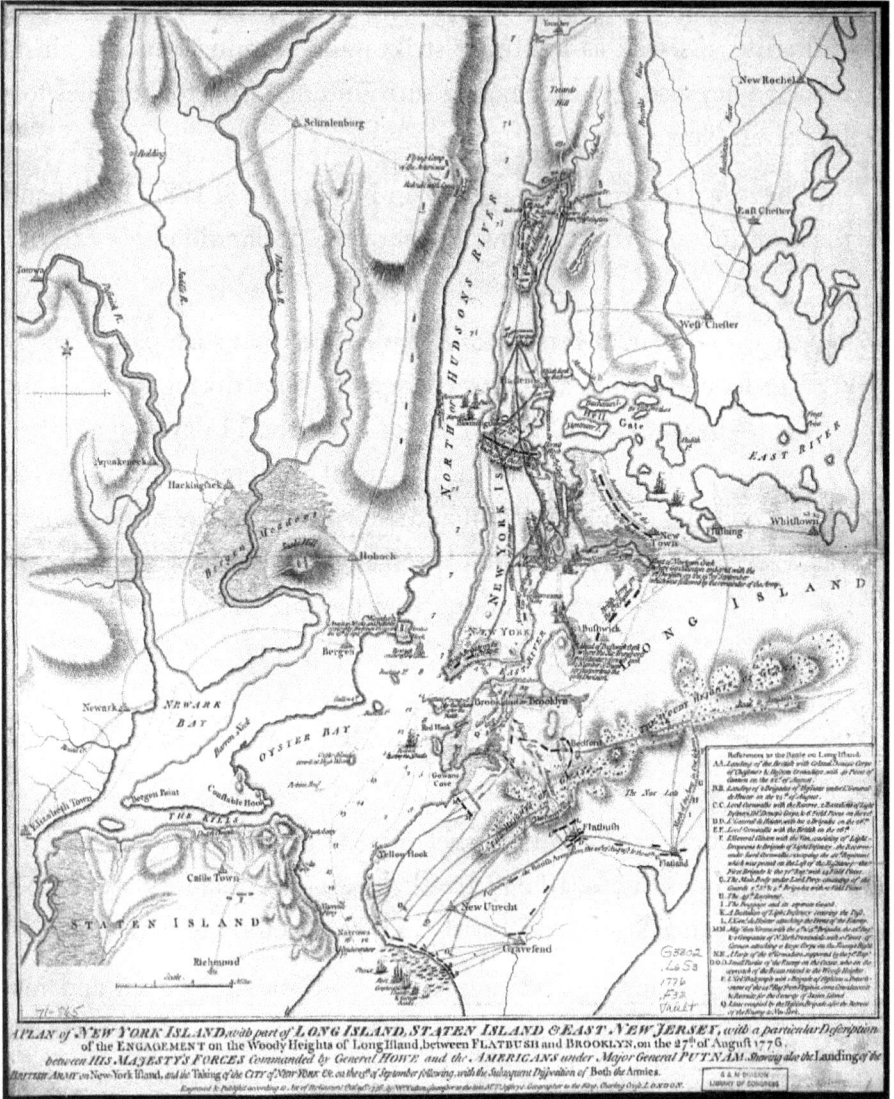

Map of New York Island, Long Island, Staten Island and East New Jersey

****

6 ENGLAND

Many thousands of American and English residents of New York and other states on the East Coast evacuated to England. They were fleeing reprisals from their fellow Americans. This flow of people started some years before the end of hostilities. Loyalists began to leave the Americas in 1774 and 1775, settling in various towns around Great Britain. Many also escaped north to British North America (now Canada). They used many East Coast ports for their journeys into exile.

January 1775 saw the refugees' first requests for aid submitted to William Legge (1731-1801), the 2nd Earl of Dartmouth, the British Secretary of State.

Most new arrivals thought this would be a temporary move, and they would later return to the colonies after Britain won the war. They had hoped to find safety and an atmosphere of tolerance in Great Britain. Naturally, like all new immigrants, they tried to live near others who had shared similar experiences.

London, 'the seat of the Empire', was a favourite town for the new arrivals to try to settle into. The districts of Westminster, Soho, Kensington, and Chelsea (favourites for New Yorkers) were popular areas for the rich to congregate.

St James's Park was a regular meeting place for Americans in London. Strolling around, seeing old friends and catching up on the latest news. Local meeting places like the Jerusalem Tavern, St. Clement's Coffee House, the New England Coffee House on Threadneedle Street, and the Adelphi Tavern on the Strand were favourite places for these exiles to meet.

"I see many faces I have been used to. America seems to be transplanted to London."
SAMUEL QUINCY, 1777

British cities like Bristol, Chester, and Warwick were other popular areas with the Americans, as well as Birmingham, which was described as a town resembling Boston by Samuel Curwen.

Times were hard for some, and they found London to be a costly place to be. Most refugees arriving had little money and had left behind their lands and families.

Loyalists wrote to their friends in America that London was "the most expensive and excessively dear place to live in that is in the whole world." In Curwen's journal, he wrote, "could not breathe the vital air without great expense."[72]

The newcomers soon found out that finding work in England was almost impossible. Even for ex-colonial officials, judges, and landowners. Professionals like doctors and lawyers soon discovered that the British did not recognise their training. Many new arrivals became destitute in England, with some becoming ill and dying in poverty. There was resentment from the English towards the newcomers. Not all local communities welcomed or accepted the Loyalists.

In later years, many refugees spread throughout the country. With many moving north to Glasgow, Scotland, a popular city with families from Virginia. The West Country and Wales were also popular destinations, and a large group moved to Chester.

There was a sizeable gathering in Bristol, where there was the most significant number of Loyalists outside the capital, as they found the cost of living nearly a third less expensive than in London.

---

[72] Samuel Curwen, Journal, pp. 61, 102.

It is 1783, and Philip is living in London, where Catharine gives birth to another daughter, Jane. Unfortunately, the little girl died two years later, in 1785.

Now, Philip starts his long battle to receive compensation for the loss of his land and goods, as he still has a large family to support.

Philip compiles a list of items lost and destroyed by American Colonialists raiding his home and lands.

His friend Major David Mathews (1739-1800), who was the 43rd and last Colonial Mayor of New York City, gave Philip a sworn letter signed on 17 September by Major Thomas Millidge (1735-1816). It was to assist Philip's claim for recompense for his farm, home, and factory.

Claims and Memorials[73]

Witness on Behalf of Philip Van Cortlandt of New Jersey.
Thomas MILLIDGE Esquire, Major of the 1st Battn. New Jersey Volunteers being duly Sworn, deposeth that he was well Acquainted with the Farm of Philip VAN CORTLAND Esquire on which he lived at Hanover and County of Morris, at the time he was driven from the same and joined His Majesty's Troops & that he thinks the sum of Twelve hundred pounds to be the just valuation of the Farm & Improvements thereon.

Also, that he had a very general knowledge of the Personal Estate of the said Philip VAN CORTLAND as mentioned in the within Estimate & is of opinion that the same is not rated beyond its real value, and that he laid before him Sundry Bonds, Mortgages & Notes amounting to the sum of One thousand one hundred and twenty-four pounds 12/1 Curt. money of New York, exclusive of any Interest thereon, & was well acquainted with the handwriting of the

---

[73] TNA. AO13. Volume 112. Folio 5.

signers, or subscribing Witnesses to the said Bonds Notes & Mortgages, except about Twenty pounds thereof.

And that he laid before him his book of Acts. including ballances due him from sundry persons in the Province of New Jersey to the amount of Six hundred eighty-seven pounds 14/7 York Curry. & that the whole sum due for said Bonds Mortgages & Books debts are due from persons in New Jersey & irrecoverably lost by Mr. CORTLAND's attainder in said Province.

(signed)   Thos. MILLIDGE
Sworn to this 17th day of September 1783
before me D MATHEWS Mayor

This letter was supported by another dated 6 October 1783, with sworn testimony from Samuel Ogden and Richard Kemble, both respected men from Morris County. The letter gave details of Philip's property, land, and value.

Samuel OGDEN Esquire late one of His Majesty's Justices of the Peace for the County of Morris in East New Jersey & Lieut. Coll. of Militia of Said County and Richard KEMBLE Esquire of Mount Kemble in the Town of Morris, in the County aforesaid being duly Sworn on the holy Evangelist of Almighty God, depose & say that they were well acquainted with the Farm of Philip VAN CORTLAND Esquire on which he lived in Hanover in the County of Morris Aforesaid at the time he was driven from the same & joined the British Army, & that they verily believe the sum of Twelve hundred pounds to be the just value thereof & the Improvements thereon.

And Also that they were well acquainted with the personal Estate on said Farm, and that they verily believe the Account of the Articles mentioned to have been thereon in the within estimate to be right and just.

And they do further say the said Farm was confiscated and sold by a law of the State of New Jersey and is now in possession of the purchaser.

Saml. OGDEN
Richd. KEMBLE
Sworn to this Sixth dayn of October 1783 before me
D Mathews MAYOR [74]

In their claims, all claimants had to prove their loyalty to the Crown and their status with sworn statements from acquaintances to help support their claims.

On November 20th, Philip sends a letter to the Commissioners. This, he followed up on the 27th with further correspondence.

To the Commissioners appointed by Act of
Parliament to enquire into the losses and services of
the American Loyalists
The memorial of Philip Van Cortland, Major of
His Majesty's 3rd Battn. New Jersey Volunteers.

Sheweth
That your Memorialist was driven by the Rebels
from his family & property in the Province of New
Jersey & joined His Majesty's army under the orders
of Sir Willm. Howe in 1776, preferring the sacrefice
of domestic happiness with the loss of fortune rather
than renounce allegiance to His Lawful Sovereign &
join in measures tending to subvert the British
Constitution.

---

[74] TNA. AO13. Volume 112. Folio 3-4.

The issue of the late unfortunate contest proves doubly distressing to your memorialist who now finds himself separated from his numerous connections, banished his native Country which was first settled by his Ancestors in a line of reputation, & with a weighty family obliged to seek an Asylum amongst Strangers which is denied him by his Countrymen.

The support of a wife and eleven children was a consideration of importance in the day of prosperity and so ill proportioned to the present circumstances of your Memorialist that he is obliged to intrude this application for such immediate relief as your wisdom shall judge adequate to his situation.

And your Memorialist will ever pray &c &c

Ph. V. Cortland   London 20th Novr. 1783.[75]

On 27 November 1783, the Army increased Philip's income after he requested assistance.

Besides his half-pay pension, they granted a further £120 a year, bringing his annual income to £300.[76] The board had considered Philip's losses in America and the fact that he had a wife and eleven children to support. They concluded the new arrangement was "to commence from midsummer 1783."

An Act of Parliament had appointed a new Committee in July 1783. They were to enquire into the losses and services of the American Loyalists.

[75] TNA. AO13. Volume 112. Folio 2.
[76] TNA. AO12. Volume 109/134 Folio 89.

This Committee, made up of five members, dealt with the Loyalists' claims. They met only every six months. The committee separated the Loyalists into six classes:

(1) Those who had rendered services to Great Britain.
(2) Those who had borne arms against the Revolution.
(3) Uniform Loyalists.
(4) Loyalists' resident in Great Britain.
(5) Those who took oaths of allegiance to American states, but afterwards joined the British.
(6) Those who took arms with the Americans and later joined the English army and navy.

It would take a long time and many years for Philip's claim to conclude and finalise. The total of his claim of losses was £8,539.6.11.

On 18 March 1784, Philip wrote from Kings Road, Chelsea, requesting asylum and relief for his losses. He attached details of his claim. [77]

Philip itemised all of his losses from Hanover. His detailed list included cattle, horses, sheep, hay, and grain. There were details of food and wine that the incoming rebel troops consumed. Also, Philip listed the tools and furniture that were lost, along with his and Catharine's, and the children's clothes. There were details about his pearl ash factory, together with a substantial claim for properties in New York and his share in the Cortlandt Manor estate. A total in sterling of £8,465.11.6.

Philip sent several letters detailing his losses, and here are some details from one of them.

An Account of Sundrys plundered from Philip Van Cortland's Family and destroyed by the Rebels before & after he was driven from his house for refusing to renounce his allegiance & to bear arms against his lawful Sov'reign, 1776- New Jersey.

---

[77] TNA AO12. Volume 22. Folio 96-.

Cattle

	£
1 Horse	30. 0. 0.
2 Mares & colts	100. 0. 0.
2 Colts	75. 0. 0.
12 Cows	72. 0. 0.
6 black cattle	36. 0. 0.
22 English Sheep & lambs	44. 0. 0.
	357. 0. 0.

Hay & Grain in barracks

17 Tons best English hay	68. 0. 0.
20 Tons bog hay	20. 0. 0.
3 loads flax	16. 10. 0.
2 loads English Oats	12. 0. 0.
25 bushells hempseed	10. 10. 0.
16 bushells flaxseed	6. 8. 0.
60 bushells wheat & rye	22. 10. 0.
2 loads wheat	16. 0. 0.
	171. 18. 0.

Provisions in Store

2 barrels choice beef	10. 0. 0.
1 Cask Gammons	8. 0. 0.
2500 bushells Turnips on 6 Acres expecting the British Troops & fell into the Rebels hands	125. 0. 0.
1 Cask old Madeira wine	20. 0. 0.
1 Cask old Mettieglin	6. 0. 0.
	169. 0. 0.

1 Cask Spirits	5. 0. 0.
2 firkins butter & hogs fat	14. 10. 0.
200 1b tallow	5. 0. 0.
110 bushells potatoes	16. 10. 0.

Cabbages, Cellory, Beets, & cask with garden seeds

	15.	0.	0.
	56.	0.	0.

Farm Tools & carriages

1 Chair & Whisky	30.	0.	0.
1 Waggon, Corn Mill & farm tools	25.	0.	0.
	55.	0.	0.

Furniture

Kitchen furniture totally	50.	0.	0.

Furniture in the house destroyed by ye Rebels most
wantonly in their nightly revels Vizt.

7 Mahogany chairs	10.	10.	0.
Branches & Andirons	2.	16.	0.
1 large family picture	15.	0.	0.
Clock & desk	15.	0.	0.
Tables & Escrutore	18.	0.	0.
Dashwood & Argyle, picture	2.	16.	0.
10 leather Chairs	7.	10.	0.
1 Spinning Wheel	0.	18.	0.
	122.	8.	0.

Children's bed cloaths	7.	0.	0.
1 Mahagonny & another chair	4.	0.	0.
1 large family dining table	10.	0.	0.

3 large loads containing wearing Apparel, bedding, servants &
Childrens cloaths plundered from his Servants at Cecaucus ferry when
they were coming to New York with Genl. Washington's pass

	325.	0.	0.

Linen, Blanketts, Gilt pictures, Mrs. Cortland's & his
Own pictures & cloaths taken near Pompton

	235.	0.	0.
	581.	0.	0.

Arms &c.

1 Fuzee & Accoutrements	6. 8. 0.
2 Musketts, Bayonets &c	6. 0. 0.
1 Drum, 3 fifes & bag flints	5. 10. 0.
1 large jug with powder	2. 12. 0.
	20. 10. 0.

Sundries

Expences for five months when obliged to furnish Rebel
Officers & Servants with provisions and drink, in the
most profuse manner during which time they destroyed a pipe
Madeira & a Cellar fill'd with liquor exclusive of that in store
250. 0. 0.

Paid for moving effects at night into Sussex for safety
66. 10. 0.

Paid moving his Family, 22 in number to New York, when
turned out of doors in a Snow Storm 40 miles from the City
79. 0. 0.
395. 10. 0.

Paid Storage & boatage on ye way	26. 10. 0.
Paid Dutch Farmers carting at night for cattle in Sussex	3. 0. 0.
Paid Guides in ye Mountains during pursuit	6. 8. 0.
Paid Expences during ditto	9. 0. 0.
30 yds wool	4. 10. 0.
	49. 8. 0.

Young Cattle & wood

Young cattle secreted with Dutch Farmers, discovered &
sold. 1 beautiful Mare, 1 horse, 3 colts, 9 heifers & Steers, with
a number of Sheep   260. 0. 0.
20 Acres wood cut down & destroye   200. 0. 0.
80 cords Wood ready cut & corded which he paid for, &

which they refused his family, tho' greatly distress'd @ 5/
Pr. Cord   20. 0. 0.
                                             480. 0. 0.

Pearl Ash manufactory
    2 large boilers   30. 0. 0.
    2 Smaller ditto   24. 0. 0.
    30 large Ash tubs   30. 0. 0.
    2 large coppers   40. 0. 0.
    3 pumps (1 copper box'd)   9. 0. 0.
    4 cisterns   12. 0. 0.
    2 hoes, 2 scrapers, hammers   5. 0. 0.
    2 cedar troughs & 4 iron grate   8. 0. 0.
    2 large iron coolers   6. 0. 0.
    1 large iron refinery   10. 0. 0.
    1 barrel pearl Ash   19. 0. 0.
2000 lives ashes in Ash house collected by Servants @ 8d Pr.
Bushel   75. 0. 0.
                                             268. 0. 0.

Debts due Philip V Cortland in New Jersey & his books
and which by means of his Attainder are irrecoverably lost
                                            1913. 6. 8.
Deduct £101 being the difference of light money
reduced to New York. Currency.   101. 0. 0.
                                            1812. 6. 8.
Farm sold in the County of Morris by Act of Assembly
with improvements in Buildings & 20 Acres bog meadows
newly ditched & reduced to English grass in high order 1200. 0. 0.
    New York Currency   £ 5788. 2. 8.

Estimate of New York Estate brought from page

(6) N York Curry.   8774. 5. 7.
                                                    £   14512. 8. 3.

Which sum reduced to sterling is   £   8465. 11. 6.[78]

Philip included with his claim extracts from the wills of William
Ricketts (1735), dated 26 July 1735, and Anne Depeyster (1774), dated
14 July 1774. Also, details from his aunt Gertrude Beekman's (1777) will
of 20 February 1776.

These details are some of his inherited property.[79] He attached a note,
"the particular value of which may be ascertained by Gentlemen of
character now in Great Britain."

One half of South lot No. 8 in ye Manor of Cortland containing
improved farms reference Mrs. Beekmans Will.
One eighth of her undivided land in sd. Manor & Rombout Patent:
being 1/8 of 1/10. 312½ acres.
One quarter of ditto in Right of Grandfather Cortlandt.
One fifth of undivided lands in Westchester County part of which
sold from 7/- to 18 Pr. Acre in Right of Grandmother Cortlandt.
One quarter of 1/10 of a Settled tract of land at Muspellan creek in
Pennsylvania.

Philip also supplied details of the house in New York that he
inherited from his mother, Mary, née Ricketts. Stating it was a two-
storey stone and brick building covered with boards.

Four rooms were on the first floor, and five were on the second level.

---

[78] TNA. AO13. Volume 112. Folios 3-6.
[79] TNA. AO12. Volume 22. Folio 108-9.

The dwelling was on John Street. Before the 'troubles', the rent was £150 p.a. The house was in good repair, and Philip valued the building as currency 4,000, or £2,250 sterling.[80]

At this time, Philip's cousin Cortland Skinner was also in Chelsea, living at 5 Fields Row.

On 24 August 1784, Philip signed a statement for the Commission of Losses verifying that he knew Mr Hake from New York and Mr Rinebeck. But he could not confirm that he knew of any land or property they owned.

In February 1785, Philip in London supported a compensation claim brought by Captain William Luce. The captain came from Elizabethtown. Philip confirmed he had known him in America and had visited his home. Which he could not value.

He believed that the captain, previously a merchant, had lost all his property during the troubles and had worked tirelessly for the crown, recruiting men and gathering military intelligence.

The Cortlandt family started moving around Britain, and it looks like Philip and his family were living in Chester and possibly staying with the Frederick Philipse family in Wervin, Chester.

Like Philip, Frederick (1720-1785) was a Loyalist and left New York in 1783. The American Congress branded him a traitor, stripped him of his birthright, and condemned him to death.

He died on 30 April 1785 and was buried in St Oswald's Parish, Chester.[81] There is a large memorial tablet on the wall at Chester Cathedral, although the date of his death on the tablet is inaccurate.

While living in Chester, Philip and Catharine had another child in May.

---

[80] TNA. AO12. Volume 22. Folio 108

[81] "England, Cheshire Parish Registers, 1538-2000, Frederick Philips, 02 May 1785, Burial; citing item 3 p 38, St Oswald, Chester, Cheshire, England, Record Office, Chester; FHL microfilm 2,068,353."

They named him William, but he died on 31 October, aged five months. They buried him on 31 October at St Oswald Churchyard, Chester, Cheshire.[82]

On 15 March 1786, Philip sent one of his first letters from his rented house on Further Northgate Street, Chester, to the Commission in London. This was requesting a speedy conclusion to his claim. He said he wished to travel to Nova Scotia that spring to start a new life for himself and his family.

To the Honorable Commission appointed by Act of Parliament for inquiring into the Losses & services of the American Loyalists
The Memorial of Philip Van Cortland late Major of his Majesty's 3rd N.J.V.

Shewith,

That upon your Memorialists' Arrival in this Kingdom upwards of two years past, he had it not then in his Power to insert in his estimate the Particulars of his Property, which was in the
Province of New York, without having reference to the map of the Manor of Cortland.
This prevented his being one of the first to present his Claim to you, and consequently to have been heard in his Turn long since.
That your Memorialist has a Wife and eleven Children who look up to him for support. That his Expenses, since he has been in this Country for their maintenance has far exceeded the Bounds of his allowance and notwithstanding the greatest
Economy he had been drove to the necessity of borrowing a large sum of money, as well as disposed of a considerable Part of his Family Plate in order to extricate him from the great Embarrassments occasioned

---

[82] "England, Cheshire Parish Registers, 1538-2000," William Van Courtland, 31 Oct 1785, Burial; citing item 3 p 39, St Oswald, Chester, Cheshire, England, Record Office, Chester; FHL microfilm 2,068,353.

by the unavoidable Expenses of his numerous Family, who have also in addition to their other Calamities been severely afflicted with sickness. Your Memorialist under these circumstances reduced from a state & affluence, to indigence submits his *own* present Feelings Feelings and Anxiety of Mind to You, in wishing to render that Paternal Care to his Children which they now depend on him for His only Mode to accomplish this desirable End is to move to Nova Scotia as early this spring as he possibly can, that he may before the Rigours of the next Winter commence, get himself somewhere settled in that Country: And unless your Memorialist can leave this Kingdom in a very short Time, and with the spring Vessels, he will not be enabled to effect his Purpose he therefore, most humbly prays, that you will take his Case under consideration and grant to him a speedy Hearing, which alone can expedite and fulfill his present Wishes. And your Memorialist as in duty bound will ever pray.

Ph V Cortland
Chester 15th March 1786 Further North Gate Street.[83]

Philip's cousin, Cortlandt Skinner, had moved from London and was living in Chester. On 30 March, he sent a letter to the Claims and Memorials Commission confirming that he knew Philip and supported Philip's claims.

Claims and Memorials

Witness on Behalf of Philip Van Cortland.

I Certify that I am well Acquainted with Majr. Philip Van Cortlandt, having known him from a boy.

---

[83] TNA. AO 13. Volume 54. Folio 651-2.

That he always declared himself in favor of
Govt. and in September 1775, When I was taken &
brought before the Committee at Morris he attended
the whole time & determinedly Spoke his opinion of
the Violence of their Conduct, particularly to Howell
who had 40 men to Guard me, advising him to be very
Carefull that no Injury was done to me.

That on my being discharged I found him placed
on the road to give me protection & advising that by
this Conduct he exposed himself to the resentment of
the Committee & their Abettors. That as soon as the
army entered Jersey, he joined me & I promised him
an appointment to a majority. That during 1777 &
Untill the Summer 1778, he continued with me acting
as my Majr. of Brigade & very often on service, witht.
any pay or reward, when he was appointed to my
fourth Battn. and put on pay & as such served Untill
the Conclusion of the war.

I further declare that Majr. Cortland always acted
openly Agt. every measure that tended to
independancy & when it was declared Cheerfully took
an Active part in support of the Authority & Govermt.
of Great Britain.

Cortd. Skinner Late Br. Genl. &c &c Prov: Forces
March 30th 1786.[84]

On 11 April, Sir Henry Clinton, supporting Philip, sent a letter from
his home in Portland Place, London, confirming that he knew him and
that he was a zealous officer serving the British Crown.

---

[84] TNA. AO12. Volume 22. Folio 101-2.

In April, Philip sent another letter to the Claims Commission and referenced the letter from his cousin, Cortlandt Skinner, that was sent in March.[85]

Philip co-signed a petition in June supporting his cousin Cortlandt Skinner and his family's claim for compensation.[86] Eight people signed the claim, including David, Isaac, and Peter Ogden and Governor Franklin.

In July, Philip's eldest daughter, Mary Ricketts, aged 22, married John McKeil Anderson in the Trinity Church, New York. She is the first of seven of his daughters to marry, and Philip and Catharine must have been disappointed not to have attended the ceremony.

Records show that in August 1786, Philip lived at 5 Rathbone Place, London, and had 11 children with him.

August 1776, and Philip wrote to Sir Evan Nepean. He was the Permanent Under-Secretary of State for the Home Department. Philip was asking for help to finalise his claim for compensation for fighting for the British in the American War of Independence. This is a copy of the letter:

Sir,

Yesterday I did myself the honor to wait on you on a subject which greatly concerns me.
About eighteen months ago you was pleased to intimate that whenever my business permitted me to leave this Country you would afford me your Assistance respecting the mode of conveying me to Nova Scotia, that period is now at hand. I find myself included in the present report of the Commissioners for Six hundred pounds & after paying the debts incurred for the necessary support of my family which was frequently aflicted with sickness, will leave me about £120 for removing to a new Country, paying passages,

---

[85] TNA. AO12. Volume 22. Folio 51.
[86] TNA. AO13. Volume 111.

purchasing stores for the voyage, exclusive furniture & cloathing of which we were deprived during the Rebellion.

Since my stay in this kingdom I have been reduced to the disagreable necessity of selling £80 Pr. An: of my half pay & have the mortification to experience my inability to redeem it under these circumstances, Sir, you will naturally suppose my anxiety awakened in behalf of a beloved family whose only Support now depends on the uncertain tenure of a single life. It was my wish to charter a vessel at Liverpool in company with a friend who has also a family at Chester, as it would be attended with less inconvenience & expence than from any other port. To accomplish this I am unable, & wretchedness must be the consequence if I am not assisted by Government.

Friendless & unknown I ask your patronage, not for myself but for a Wife & eleven children, who have suffered for my principles of Loyalty, & whose early days were marked with more pleasing prospects.

Pardon this freedom & impute any impropriety to its proper cause.

I have the honor to be with assured respect

Sir Your Most Obedt.

Ph. V. Cortland

No. 5 Rathbone Place   4th Augt. 1786

Sir Guy Carlton, Lord Dorchester, forwarded his letter and his support to the Claims Commission.

Major Cortland's conduct has been very meritorious & I have every reason to think his representation is true, & think him deserving of favour.

Dorchester   August 12th 1786 [87]

Mr Nepean enclosed his comments and forwarded Philip's and Lord Dorchester's correspondence for further action.

Whitehall 12 August 1786.

Sir,

I transmit to you herewith a Letter to me from Major Cortland, to which is annexed a note written by Ld. Dorchester, and I am directed by Lord Sydney to desire you will lay the same before the Lords Commissioners of His Majesty's Treasury and that you will recommend Major Cortland's case to their Lordship's favorable consideration.

I am Sir

Your most obedient

humble servant

Evan Nepean [88]

Later, in 1786, Philip received £1,500 from the Claims Commission [89] for his New York property, although his total claim amounted to £8,539.

Because of his loyalty to the crown, Philip had lost his considerable estate in Hanover and his New York properties. Under the confiscation laws passed by all the states, the new revolutionary government had the authority to seize Loyalists' land and property. The Patriots repossessed all of Philip's property in Morris County. On June 8, 1778, they sold part for £156.5.6d.

---

[88] TNA AO13. Volume 112. Folio 18.
[89] TNA. AO12. Volume 109.

On March 31, 1779, they sold the remaining property for £3293.1.6d, Continental money, a bitter pill for Philip to swallow.[90]

The British government had promised land grants to Loyalists who had to leave America.

As life for Philip and the family was getting dire in England, they decided to travel to Nova Scotia. Philip could not find useful employment or funds to support his family, and he was still waiting to hear about his claims. He also put in a claim for help in paying the passage fees for his family.

Philip had hoped to charter the vessel 'Necefsaryo'[91] with a loyalist family, but did not have the funds to do this. Still, the authorities were very slow in deciding his case. Philip sent another letter.

To the Commissioners
appointed by Act of
Parliament for enquiring
into the losses & services
of the American Loyalists

The memorial of Philip Van Cortland late of New Jersey & Major of His Majests 3d Battn. New Jersey Volunteers

Most respectfully Sheweth

That Your Memorialist intends as soon as possible to embark for Nova Scotia where he proposes to settle himself & family, he therefore requests your permission for that purpose, & that you will be pleased to allow his Atty. Charles Cooke Esqr. to receive on his Acct. whatever money may be granted to him by Government under your report.

---

[90] TNA. AO13. Volume 83.
[91] TNA. AO12. Volume 103. Folio a78

And as Your Memorialist now finds himself reduced in his circumstances to a State very little removed from indigence he prays that his Allowance of £120 Pr. An. may be continued, to him.

Ph. V. Cortland[92]

Philip was offered a passage on another ship from Liverpool. He was still on military half-pay. And had to accept a loan from a friend of £150 to pay for the journey.

On 6/7th Sept 1786,[93] Philip, Catharine and nine children sailed from Liverpool to Shelbourne, Nova Scotia. The journey should have taken 35 days. Another twist of fate in his life was that the ship they were sailing on hit awful weather and had to shelter in a large bay in the Isle of Man for two weeks.

On the 5th of the month, there were reports of an earthquake being felt in Lisbon, Portugal. A few days later, tremors were also felt in Cumberland. The rest of the month had regular reports of heavy rain and storms.

Their ship recommenced its journey on the 22nd but had to run to shelter in Bristol owing to strong westerly winds. This was not the end of their troubles. The storms kept coming, and the ship struggled on its journey.

After some 95 days at sea, the vessel and the Cortlandt family finally arrived in Funchal, Madeira. They all arrived there safely around the 10th of December. Their journey had cost them dear. Most of their belongings were either lost or damaged, and Catherine, pregnant, was in poor health. Philip's distraught family left the ship and tried to find shelter and support. The vessel they had all arrived on then departed Madeira on the 14th of December to complete its journey to Nova Scotia.

---

[92] TNA. AO13. Volume 112. Folio 12.
[93] TNA. AO13. Volume 112 part 11.

Philip was almost destitute and lacked the funds to continue the family's journey across the Atlantic.

His only recourse was to contact Charles Murray, the British Consul General on the island. To ask for help for his family and the assistance of the charity of strangers.

Mr Murray, a Scot, was a wine trader for Scott, Pringle, Cheap & Co, and the British Consul since his appointment in 1771. Charles Murray was the British Consul until 1801. Mr Murray had previously travelled extensively in the colonies and sided with the interests of the colonialists.

Philip also arranged for his solicitor, Charles Cooke, in London, to contact the authorities there for help.

Philip's last son, Arthur Auchmuty, was born in March 1787 whilst the family were in Funchal, Madeira. On the families' return to England some years later, they baptised Arthur, aged 12 years 2 months, at St Mary's Church, Guys Cliffe, Warwickshire, on 10 May 1799.

The village is situated about halfway between Warwick and Kenilworth in Warwickshire, England, and the church, first founded in 1123 by Roger de Newburgh, the Earl of Warwick, is still in regular use today. Like his siblings, Arthur served in the British army. He was a captain in the 45th Nottinghamshire Regiment and died in India. He never married.

On 16 April, Charles Cooke sent a letter to the Honourable Commissioners enquiring into the losses and sufferings of the American Loyalists. This was requesting relief for the family.

> To the Honourable
> Commissioners appointed
> by Act of Parliament for
> enquiring into the Losses
> and Sufferings of the
> American Loyalists &c
> &c &c

The Memorial of Major Philip Van Cortland by Charles Cooke his Attorney

Sheweth,

That your Memorialist's Circumstances were so reduced before he left this Kingdom by Reason of the necessary Support for a numerous Family, that he was under the absolute Necessity of selling the greatest Part of the Pay arizing on his Commission of a Majority in one of the late Corps raised in America.

That your Memorialist being thus situated and anxious to remove with his Family to Nova Scotia, he made an Application to the Lords of the Treasury in the month of August last for some aid to enable him to pay his Passage to that Country, which your Memorialist was informed had been referred to the Consideration of your Honourable Board; but as an opportunity offered from Liverpool just at that Time, your Memorialist thought best to embrace it, and he embarked before you made your Report, being assisted by a Friend with the Loan of £150 to defray his necessary Expences for the Voyage, without which he could not have departed from this Kingdom. That on the 7th September last he, with his Family left Liverpool for the port of Shelburne in Nova Scotia, and by Reason of violent Storms, the Vessel was obliged to put into the Isle of Man for Safety, where she remained until the 22nd of that month, when she again sailed for her destined Port. That after

contending with Tempests and Head Winds for 95 Days, the Vessel about the 10th December was obliged to put into the Island of Madeira for Supplies.

That your Memorialist's Wife being then dangerously Ill, and in a Situation not fit to proceed with the Vessel on her Voyage, she sailed again on the 14ᵗʰ of said December, leaving your Memorialist and Family there to be dependent upon the Charity of Strangers for Support. That your Memorialist is now under the disagreeable Apprehensions of not having an Opportunity of a Passage to Nova Scotia from Madeira, without a circuitous Voyage for that Purpose, and his distressed Circumstances will not enable him to effect it unless through the assistance and Benevolence of others; he therefore prays, that you will take his and Family's Situation under Consideration, and grant him such Relief as to you shall seem proper.

And your Memorialist as in Duty bound will ever pray—

Charles Cooke

London 16ᵗʰ April 1787[94]

Some help was granted to Philip with a grant of £100 on 17 May 1787,[95] paid to Philip's agent in England, Mr Charles Cooke.

In Madeira on 25 April, Catharine, Philip's third daughter, married Dr William Gourlay. William was a physician and wrote a book on natural history, climate, and diseases of Madeira.

On 12 June 1787, an article appeared in the Chester Courier under the heading "A Case of extreme distress." The Manchester Mercury also published the article on the 19ᵗʰ.

It was an appeal to "the benevolence of friends and others" to gather funds to assist the Van Cortlandt family in Madeira in continuing their journey to Nova Scotia.

The families' circumstances were dire, and Catherine was expecting a new baby. They needed means to pay for the voyage to Nova Scotia via Lisbon and possibly to London.

---

[94] TNA. AO13. Volume 112. Folio 8-9.
[95] TNA. AO12. Volume 102. Folio 77.

A Cafe of extreme Diftrefs.

MAJOR PHILIP VAN CORTLAND, a Gentleman once poffeffed of a handfome independent Property, befides very confiderable Expectations from his Family, was among the Number of thofe, who, by a fteady Adherence to their Loyalty, and active Exertions in Arms towards fuppreffing the late Revolt in North America, have been totally deprived of Fortune and Profpects, and obliged to take refuge in Britain.

Mr. Cortland for fome Time took up his Refidence at Chefter, with a Refignation to his narrowed Circumftances that gained the efteem of all who knew him: But his Difficulties increafing, he at length determined to remove his large Family to one of his Majefty's Colonies, where he might form fome Plan for their fupport. He accordingly embarked, with a Wife and nine Children, at Liverpool, in September laft, for Nova Scotia;—but was firft obliged to difpofe of the greateft Part of his Half-pay (the Reward of Military Services) to defray the Expences of the Voyage.

This was his laft miferable Refource.—But his ill Fortune ftill purfued him, and with redoubled Severity. He was foon overtaken with a Storm, and this was followed by a Succeffion of many others, fo extremely violent, that the Veffel was frequently in the moft imminent Danger of foundering—and became in fact a Wreck at Sea. But, moft providentially, the Major and the reft who were on Board, after being toffed about for ninety-five Days, and experiencing the moft dreadful Sufferings (their whole Store of Provifions being nearly exhaufted) reached at length a Port in the Ifland of Madeira. There the Major now remains with his large Family—and the profpect of another Child being very foon added to it!—oppreffed with Sicknefs and with Poverty.

He depends, for his own fubfiftence, and that of his Wife and Nine Children, on the bounty of Strangers. This cannot laft long, and yet he is utterly unable, for want of Money, to purfue his Voyage to Nova-Scotia, which cannot probably be done without going firft to Lifbon, or returning to England. This will require a confiderable Sum of Money; and unlefs the Benevolence of his Friends, and Others, enables him to raife that Sum, he and his Family muft be in no fmall Danger of perifhing for want on the Ifland of Madeira!

⁎ Contributions for this unfortunate Family will be received by Meff. Bidulph, Cox, and co Bankers, at Charing-crofs, and by Meff. Gofling, Bankers, Fleet-ftreet London; at Chefter, by Mr. Speed, in the Abby Square; at Liverpool by the Rev. G. Hodfon, Duke Street; and at Manchefter by the Rev. H. Owen, in Ridge field.

COMMERCIAL FAIRS.

Philip and the family travelled to Halifax, Nova Scotia, in 1788. But there are no records of the vessel they sailed on or when they departed Madeira.

In May 1788, Philip was granted 300 acres of land by the Tuskett River.

On the 19th, John Parr, the governor of Nova Scotia, issued a warrant for the survey of land on behalf of Philip and 40 others on 12,150 acres by the Tuskett River in the County of Shelburne. Philip's interest was 200 acres.[96]

The following day, Philip's attorney in London wrote to the Commissioners enquiring into the Losses and Services of the American Loyalists. He advised them that Philip and his family were now in Halifax in Nova Scotia, and they were in desperate need of money.

This is a copy of his letter.

To the Commissioners appointed by Act of Parliament for enquiring into the Losses and Services of the American Loyalists.

Respectfully Sheweth

That Philip Van Cortland is now at Halifax in Nova Scotia in want of Money with a Numerous and expensive Family to Support, & the Necessaries of life very dear. That Michael Kearney is at present in New Jersey with a Wife and upwards of Seven Children, where he has been detained contrary to his wishes by indisposition, but proposes to remove to the Province of New Brunswick the beginning of this Month, to reside permanently.

That William Luce is, your Memorialist believes, a Captain of a British Merchant Vessel Trading to the different West India Islands

---

[96] Nova Scotia Archives; Halifax, Nova Scotia, Canada; *Nova Scotia Land Petitions (1765-1800)*; Volume Number: *2/144*.

belonging to the British Government & your Memorialist believes he is in want of Cash, & not in a very lucrative Employment. Therefore, your Memorialist very Respectfully Prays that you may [be] pleased to continue Philip Van Cortland's leave of absence from 5 Jany. last & the leaves of Michael Kearney & William Luce from 5 July 1787,

the respective Periods in which they have Ceased.

And your Memorialist shall &c.

Charles Cooke,   London 20th May 1788[97]

Now, the family was in Halifax. In May, Margaret Hughes, Philip's fourth daughter, married Captain O. Elliott Ovens-Elliott (1761-17 March 1811). He was an Englishman from Binfield Park in Berkshire, England and was serving with the 57th Foot Regiment stationed in Nova Scotia.

The following year, Catherine, aged 43, gave birth to her last child, Sophia Sawyer (1789-1841), in Halifax, Nova Scotia. After the family returned to England and on 13 October 1814, Sophia married Captain Sir William Howe Mulcaster (1783-1837) in Duloe, Cornwall. She died in Wyke Regis at her sister-in-law Ann's home.

This was a busy year for the family as their daughter, Gertrude, on 15 March 1789 in Halifax, Nova Scotia, married Capt. Edward Buller (1764-1824), a captain in His Majesty's Navy from Trenant Park, Cornwall, England.

On 23 March 1790, Philip sent a letter to the Nova Scotia governor, John Parr. He requested the allocation of a tract of land for his family. It was a lot of land, approximately 2,000 acres, which the government had previously given to Major and Peter Trail.

This land on the road between Horton and Annapolis had now been Escheated (returned to the government).

---

[97] TNA AO13. Volume 112. Folio 10.

On 3 May, Philip sent another letter with a little more detail. He asked for his previous request to be granted. They approved his request.

Records from the Crown Land Office in Halifax show that on 31 December 1790, details of land grants in Aylesford Township, Kings County, Nova Scotia, that the government granted and surveys completed.

Philip Van Cortland

1790

Kings, Nova Scotia, Canada

Major of H.M late 3rd Batt. New Jersey Volunteers. Memorials (2). Warrant to Survey. Surveyor's Certificate. Surveyor's Report: 2600 acres. Township of Aylesford. Bounded in part by the western boundary of Cornwallis. County of Kings. For further details, see Report. List of Major Van Cortland's family: Major Philip Van Cortland & Wife — 1050 acres. Ensign Philip Van Cortland, Jr. — 500 acres, Ensign Jacob Ogden Van Cortland — 500 acres. 550 acres divided among the following: Van Cortland, Stephen Van Cortland, Elizabeth Van Cortland, Arthur Achmuty Van Cortland, Mary Ricketts Van Cortland, Catherine Van Cortland, Gertrude Van Cortland, Charlotte Van Cortland, Sophia Sawyer Van Cortland, Henry Clinton Van Cortland, Margt. Van Cortland, Sarah Memorials (2) Warrant to Survey. Surveyor's Certificate. Surveyor's Report.

The English government fulfilled their promise and granted Philip and his family land in the township of Aylesford, Nova Scotia, where he later built his summer residence.

Aylesford is situated west of Cornwallis and Horton by the border of Wilmot Township in the county of Annapolis.

The Annapolis and Kings County Land Grants Map 35 shows that Van Cortlandt's land was in Area 8. This covered Berwick West, Berwick, Factorydale, Somerset and Weston.

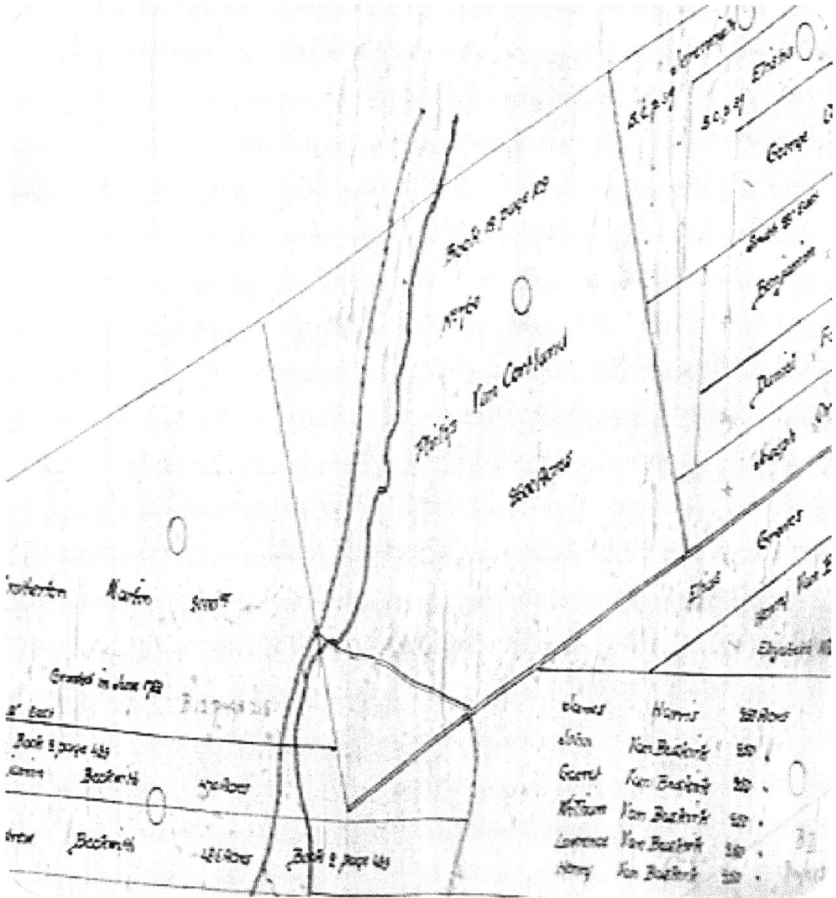

Philip's land was in Aylesford in Western Kings County in the Annapolis Valley.

The Cornwallis town border bordered the land in the north and Brotherton Martin and Benjamin Beckwith's land to the east. A river and a road ran through the land.

The land grant,[98] 2,600 acres, issued on 31 December 1790 and signed by the Nova Scotia governor, John Parr, came with strict conditions. A yearly ground rent of 2/- per 100 acres had to be paid to the state on 29 September, the feast of St. Michael.

This land grant stated that the payment of the rent would begin 10 years after the state issued the original grant.

The clause in the agreement showed that failure to pay the amount would result in the crown regaining ownership of the land. Also, within three years, the land granted had to be cleared and then cultivated. A house at least 20 ft (6.1 m) in length and 16ft (4.88 m) in breadth had to be built.

Now that Philip and the family have received land, he starts to build a new life. He is still on a limited income and writes to influential friends in 1790 regarding monies owed to him from assets sold by the Cortlandt family. They have only paid him a small proportion of the funds due.[99]

In the final report of the Claims Commission 1790, they stated they had received 3,225 claims from England and Canada.

It identified that 2,291 Loyalists had received £3,033,091.00 in compensation. But this figure was considerably lower than the losses the Loyalists had claimed.

On 6 May 1791, Philip and Catherine's second daughter, Elizabeth, married William Taylor. The ceremony took place in Cowley, Gloucestershire, with Thomas Nash conducting the service. Her sister Margaret Hughes and brother-in-law O. Elliott Ovens were the witnesses. Again, Philip could not attend the wedding, as he was in Nova Scotia.

---

[98] NSA. Crown Land Old Book 19. p.109.

[99] van Cortlandt, Philip, Dec. 30, 1790, bak00226c00063d. Baker Library Special Collections and Archives, Harvard Business School.

To support his family, Philip, and some friends formed an import and export shipping business. They would export fish and shingles to the West Indies and Madeira and import goods and rum back to Halifax.

On 14 Jun 1791, Philip wrote to the General Assembly of the Province of Nova Scotia in Halifax regarding a shipment of codfish, barrels of pickled fish and shingles to the West Indies and returning with a cargo of rum.

He requested an exemption from tax on the shipments. There had been problems and delays with the shipments, with some of the cargo had to be returned to Halifax.[100]

In 1793, Governor Sir John Wentworth (1737-1820), who had arrived on Sunday, 13 May 1792, in Halifax after a six-week passage from Falmouth, was worried about a French attack on the town. Reports received stated that the French fleet had anchored in New York Bay.

There was much discontent in Europe after the French Revolution and the establishment of the First French Republic in 1792, which caused the outbreak of war in 1793. This new government was a threat to many countries. In February 1793, France declared war on Great Britain and the Netherlands, and hostilities began after Russia, European states, and the British formed a coalition against the French.

In London, the Secretary of State, Henry Dundas, sent a dispatch to provincial governors. He advised, "take the necessary steps for raising and forming from amongst the inhabitants. a corps not exceeding 600 men, to be divided into six companies, with the usual establishment of commissioned and non-commissioned officers." He also gave instructions that these units were to serve as Fencible units for home defence only.

Wentworth received the notice from London in April and immediately requested counties to supply troops for a provincial force.

---

[100] Nova Scotia Archives RG 5 Series A volume 4, numbers 14 and 16.

Philip raised a company of men in King's County. Along with others, they moved to Melville Island, a small peninsula that was located in the Northwest Arm of Halifax Harbour.

In 1797, the documentation shows that Philip had left the militia.

With his shipping partner Jonathan Tremain, an ex-New Yorker, in June 1795, they sent a request to the Governor at the House of Assembly for an exemption of duty on import tax on rum they had brought to Halifax.

Philip and his family returned to England and travelled to Warwick. They stayed at Guys Cliff House, a grand manor house owned by Bertie Greatheed in Warwickshire. Bertie's father, Samuel, who had previously rented the property, purchased the house in 1750. When Bertie travelled abroad, which he did regularly, he would also rent out the house.

In September 1798, Philip's daughter, Margaret Hughes, and her husband stayed at Guys Cliff. While there, Onesiphorus obtained a Game certificate.

Philip, in January 1799, wrote to his cousin Philip at the Cortlandt Manor in America. He was trying to reconcile the family rift.

He said,

"No gratification can be so pleasing to me as that which will result from your favoring me with a letter to mention the return of friendship between us, tis a wish nearest my heart: & tho' tis decreed that I must be separated from my Native Country I am less anxious for its prosperity, nor for the welfare of those once dear to me."[101]

His cousin never responded.

****

---

[101] Guys Cliff, Warwick. 5 January, 1799. New York Public Library.

7 FINAL MOVE

After the Amiens Treaty of 1802 failed, the British government declared war on France the following year. The authorities, fearing an attack by the French, began strengthening the English coastal defences. They instructed the construction of a network of redoubts (forts) and smaller Martello towers. The Barracks Office in London authorised the building of 103 towers that stretched along the coast from Aldeburgh, Suffolk, to Seaford in Sussex. After completion of the works, there were 74 Martello towers built along the coast between Folkestone, Kent and Seaford, Sussex. The government also planned to construct additional military barracks to protect the South Coast.

It's 1803. Philip has been on half-pay from the military and an unattached officer for many years. The Barrack Master General, Oliver DeLancey Jnr (1749–1822), a fellow American, offers him a commission as Barrack Master. This would be at the new barracks in Hailsham, in the county of Sussex, on the south coast of England.

Oliver DeLancey Jnr was an American educated in England who served in the American War of Independence. He was the second son of Brigadier General Oliver Delancey Snr (1718–1785). During the war, his father led the Delancey Brigade, which defended Long Island, New York.

Junior had served in the British army since 1766. He rose to the rank of general. Later, Oliver's superiors promoted him to lieutenant-colonel in the adjutant general's department. After the war, the king offered him a Letter of Service. Delancey Jnr took charge of settling loyal Americans' compensation claims in London. King George III had appointed Oliver after Lord Sydney recommended him.

The king also offered him the new Superintendent General of Barracks position in 1794.

His brother, Stephen, had served as a lieutenant-colonel in the 2nd battalion of New Jersey Volunteers.

Oliver's grandmother's maiden name was Anne Van Cortlandt, a different branch of the family from Philip. It helps to have friends in high places!

Since returning to England from Nova Scotia in the late 1700s, this was to be Philip's last move. He would settle in the small Sussex market town a few miles from the southern coast of England.

The town lying between Lewes, Pevensey Castle, and Eastbourne, with its Redoubt fortress and with its new barracks built on common land, would cause some disruption. As would the encamped troops, as they would double the town's population. Hailsham had about 900 residents at this time, no squire or overlord. In fact, the local traders and the church were the 'elite', with most traders owning their own property and, in some cases, additional dwellings that they let out. The nearest families of note were in Eastbourne or the Gage's, Philip's cousins, in Firle House, Firle, Sussex.

Philip and family rented a large house from Mrs Mary Sly (née Bristow). She had recently inherited the building named 'Newlands'. It was an extensive property with an adjoining paddock on George Street. A fine building set on eight acres of land and built in 1793. The house facing south had stables and a coach house at the rear.

There were two parlours, a housekeeper's room and servants' quarters in the attic. Opposite the house were open fields and fine views over the Pevensey Flats. The Cortlandt family raised chickens, pigs, and many ducks on this land. They also planted grain in the nearby field.

William Strickland, a successful local business owner and Justice of the Peace, some years later, in 1881, purchased the building for £1,250. He enlarged the premises by adding a new wing on either side of the house. Then, he renamed the building 'Cortlandt' in memory of Philip. This building is now a Grade II listed structure.

The 23rd Royal Welch Fusiliers received a posting to Hailsham in April 1804. Lieutenant Jacob Van Cortlandt, Philip's second son, was one of their officers. It is conjectured that Jacob's regiment billeted him with his father. The regiment returned in 1807 after Jacob had received a promotion to captain. Unfortunately, Jacob got injured while fighting on the Spanish/Portuguese border on 27 September 1811 and died of his wounds.

Although living in a small town in Sussex, Catharine, and Philip regularly travelled to London, a journey by stagecoach of sixty-four miles. The pickup point in Hailsham was at the Crown Inn, on the High Street.

Stagecoaches used to travel about five miles per hour, so quite a journey for a not-so-young Catharine and Philip as the stagecoach left Hailsham at 8 am on Mondays, Wednesdays and Fridays, arriving early evening some ten hours later in London. The return journey was on Tuesdays, Thursdays and Saturdays, departing at 7.30 am and arriving in Hailsham at about 6 pm. The Eastbourne to London coach terminated at the Golden Cross Inn, Charing Cross. They demolished the inn after the 1826 Charing Cross Act because of the development of the new celebratory Trafalgar Square. The new square opened to the public in May 1844.

There were three companies operating services to London, one of them to 93 Bishopsgate Street, so they probably used different companies depending on where in London they wished to visit.

It looks like Philip and Catharine also travelled to other towns in England. On 17 October 1806, there was a grand music festival held in Chester. Philip and Catherine attended the event.

In a diary left by a local Hailsham farmer, Matthias Slye, he gives us some helpful information from 1808.

"Sometimes Kitty would travel alone and, on the 14 February, she went to London." Another entry advises that Philip returned from town on 31 May, and Kitty returned on 2 August. "On 18 August, she and Philip travelled together and returned on 17 September."

Presumably, Philip was on summer military leave. There must have been a large celebration on their return, as records show that ten lambs were purchased from Matthias Slye for the grand price of 14/- each. Another entry in the diary says, "On 29 September, Kitty travelled again to London." This appears to be the only surviving record of their travels. However, they must have regularly travelled to the surrounding towns, although there are no records of any journeys.

The Hailsham barracks were in continuous use from when they opened in 1804 until their closure in 1815. Over thirty different regiments passed through the town during its existence. There are no records of anything unusual happening to the family during the time the barracks were open.

After all the trials and tribulations of Philip's earlier life, he seems to have had a settled and quiet life in Sussex. Whilst in Hailsham, he was a firm supporter of the parish church.

In 1809, Philip wrote to the Barrackmaster-General's Office asking for funds to purchase his rented house. The owner, Mrs Slye, wanted to sell the property. They refused his request[102], and on 4 May 1812, the house Philip occupied was auctioned.

On Sunday, 1 May 1814, Philip died at his home in Hailsham after a short but severe illness. In April 1814, Philip had made his will, and his executors proved it in London on 4 July 1814.[103]

---

[102] TNA. WO46. Volume 122.
[103] TNA. PROB11/1559

They buried Philip on 18 May in the local church, St Mary, where they erected a memorial that now hangs on the church wall. The plaque states he was a Colonel.

In
Memory of
COLONEL PHILIP
VAN CORTLANDT,
of the MANOR of
CORTLANDT.
A RETIRED ROYALIST
officer
of The AMERICAN War,
DIED at HAILSHAM,
MAY, 1814,
Aged 74 years.
"The Memory of the Just
is Blessed." Prov, X, VII.

Many years later, when the church was undergoing renovations, repairing damage caused by bombing during the Second World War, they moved Philip's body 6ft further into the church.

We do not know if Catherine was unhappy living in Hailsham.

She would have had little in common with her neighbours, considering her background and after such a traumatic life. Shortly after her husband's death, she moved to Devon with her youngest daughter, Sarah. They stayed with her other daughter, Lady Gertrude Buller.

On the 2nd and 3rd of June 1814, a local agent, Verrall and Sons, auctioned the Cortlandt's personal possessions. The sale included all the Van Cortlandt family's furniture. Their household items, a small library of books, and timber. As well as their collection of animals, which included 60 ducks, a sow, pigs and a few chickens. Also included in the sale was a granary, poultry house and produce from two meadows.

Even though Philip had arranged to leave his land holdings in North America and Nova Scotia to Catharine in his will, she made a trip to the Channel Islands in February 1816. Where she sought help from Lieutenant Governor Major-General Sir Hugh Mackay Gordon, an old family friend who had served in the American War of Independence.

Their meeting was to assist in securing a widow's pension. On 13 February, in Guernsey, she signed a statement requesting a pension.[104] Captain Howe Mulcaster, her son-in-law, signed an additional form to confirm and certify the details.

On 22 June in Jersey, she signed a further statement requesting a pension. This was co-signed by the Governor, who forwarded it to the War Office.[105] The Governor also sent a message confirming that he had known the family for some years.

---

[104] TNA. WO42 Volume 63. Folio 264.
[105] TNA. WO42 Volume 63. Folio 263.

The War Office granted Catharine a £130 pension shortly afterwards.[106] In 1817, they increased this by granting Sarah Ogden and Charlotte a small allowance from the Compassionate Fund.[107]

On 9 July 1819, Catherine's daughter, Catharine Gourlay, died, and they buried her in the British cemetery in Madeira.[108]

While living with her daughter Gertrude in Devon, Catherine passed away on 22 February 1828, aged 81. They buried her in the St. Andrew's Churchyard, Torre, Torquay, Devon. The church has a memorial to Catharine set in the floor. Times change, and the church is now known as St. Andrew's Greek Orthodox Church.

---

[106] TNA. WO55/1856.WO40/26.
[107] TNA. WO25/3083.
[108] Madeira British Consulate Register of Burials in British Cemetery 1809-1837. 93.

Her daughters, Sarah, Charlotte and son, Philip, were the executors of the will written in 1824. They proved Catharine's will in London on 12 April.[109]

After leaving America and receiving half pay from the army, Philip tried to secure employment. And find a home in which to settle. But he was unsuccessful until he accepted the position of Barrack Master in Hailsham.

For some years, the family travelled around England. They stayed with different relatives and sometimes rented properties. The family had also travelled to Nova Scotia to start a new life, but could not settle there.

Catharine and Philip had a large family with seventeen children that we know of. However, on Catharine's death, only seven children, two sons and five daughters, were still living.

In May 1832, the surviving members of Philip's family in England, his son Philip, his wife Mary, Gertrude Buller, Sarah Ogden, Charlotte, and Sophia and her husband William Mulcaster, sold their interests in the lands in Nova Scotia. They sold the land to Pringle Taylor, Elizabeth's son. The amount agreed was £400, British currency.[110]

That is about £57,300 in today's value. Because of his service in India, Henry Clinton could not sign the agreement when it was drawn up.

****

---

[109] TNA. PROB11. Volume 1739. Folio.138.

[110] NSA.Kings County Register of Deeds. Book 24 p.185. folio 181-192.

8 CHILDREN

As an American and a man of conscience with a strong allegiance to the British Crown, Philip, and Catherine's lives changed drastically. Disowned by his family in America and having lost all his estates and businesses, he had to forge a new life in a foreign land. But what of his children?

Mary Ricketts 1763-1807

Philip and Catharine's first child, a daughter, was born in Jamaica, New York City, in 1763. Catharine was just sixteen years old, and they named the child Mary Ricketts.

Mary married John McNeil Anderson (1758-1804) of Maryland on 10/11 July 1784 in Trinity Church, New York.

They had seven children: Mary Anne Anderson (1789-1839) /Young, Lieutenant John McNeil Anderson (1791-1814), Major Philip Cortlandt Anderson (1793-24 April 1842), James Anderson (1796-), Elizabeth Elliot Anderson (1799-18 July 1865) /Trotter, Catherine Ogden Anderson (1 June 1801-25 Jan 1863),[111] /Angelo and Margaret Maria Douglas Anderson (19 March 1804-21 May 1874)[112] /Freer. Mary died in 1807.

---

[111]

https://www.findagrave.com/memorial/262017959/catharine-ogden_van_cortlandt-angelo: accessed 30 January 2024.
[112] Find a Grave Memorial ID 108149992, citing Cimetière Mont-Royal, Outremont, Montreal Region, Quebec, Canada;

Elizabeth 1764-22 July 1816

Philip and Catharine's second child, also a daughter, was born in 1764 on Long Island and named Elizabeth.

Aged 27, Elizabeth, in 1786, married William Taylor (17 March 1746-16 August 1806) in Cowley, Gloucestershire, on 6 May 1791.[113] Her sister, Margaret Hughes, and her husband, O. Elliott Ovens-Elliott, were witnesses. Before the outbreak of hostilities, William was a lawyer in Middletown, New Jersey, the town where he was born.

They had six children: 4 boys and 2 girls. John William (born 1792, died in command of the Dacca Provisional Battalion, known to alive in 1806), Major General Joseph Pringle Taylor (25 January 1796-5 April 1884), George Elliott Taylor (1790-8 Feb 1833), Colonel Cortlandt Taylor (13 May 1798-19 June 1874), Catharine-Eliza (1795-4 Apr 1830)[114] /Moore. and Susan-Helen, (dates unknown).

Because of the war, William lost all his land in Perth Amboy but later returned to America and repurchased his estates.

The Commission in London granted him a pension of £130 p.a.[115] William died on 16 August 1806 in Perth Amboy, Middlesex County, New Jersey. Ten years later, Elizabeth, on 22 July 1816, died in Perth Amboy, Middlesex County, New Jersey, and her body was laid to rest in Saint Peter's Churchyard.[116]

---

[113] GM:61/488.
[114] Trinity Church Cemetery and Mausoleum, Manhattan, New York County, New York, USA.
[115] TNA. AO12. Volume 109.
[116] Find a Grave Memorial ID 162572208, citing Saint Peters Churchyard, Perth Amboy, Middlesex County, New Jersey, USA;

Catharine 1764–July 1819

Twin of Elizabeth, Catharine married Dr William Gourley (1766-18 Nov 1827) of Kincraig, Scotland, on 25 April 1787, in Madeira.

He was a physician at the British Factory in Madeira. Also, he was known as an amateur naturist. There was an announcement of their marriage in the Chester newspapers, where the Van Cortlandt family had recently lived.

They had 5 children, John (?-29 Dec 1833),[117] Catharine (-Dec 1864), /Douglas/Bean, Elizabeth, Jean Plenderleath (-1823) /Austin, and Gertrude Buller (-4 June 1847).[118]

Catharine died, and they interned her on the island of Madeira on 9 July 1819.[119] Her husband returned to Scotland.

Philip 30 July 1766-1 Oct 1833

In 1766, Catharine gave birth to twin boys whilst on Long Island, New York.

Young Philip, as a teenager, enlisted as an ensign and joined his father in the New Jersey Volunteers in 1780.

Philip married Mary Addison (1768?1781-17 Jan 1835) on 16 Sept 1817 in Saint Andrew's Church, Québec.[120] They had a son, George W, who died young.

After the evacuation of New York in 1783, Philip became a lieutenant in the Royal Nova Scotia Regiment.

---

[117] Perthshire Courier. 6 February 1834,
[118] Perthshire Advertiser 1 July 1847.
[119] Madeira British Consulate Register of Burials in British Cemetery 1809-1837. 93.
[120] Ancestry.com. Quebec, Vital and Church Records (Drouin Collection), *1621-1967* [database online]. Provo, UT, USA: Ancestry.com Operations Inc, 2008.

He then transferred to the Royal Newfoundland Regiment in October 1795 until it disbanded in July 1802. He joined the Newfoundland Fencible Infantry as a captain in August 1803. In 1806, this became the Royal Newfoundland Fencibles Infantry.

In 1811, Philip served as the Town Major of Halifax. On 20 February 1813, he received the appointment of Deputy Barrack Master in Halifax, Nova Scotia.[121]

Philip died at his home in St. Michael's Terrace, near Devonport, Devon, England, on 1 October 1833, and was buried on the 7th. In his last will, written on 7 August 1828 in Québec and proved in London on 12 December 1833, Philip bequeathed all his interests to his wife, Mary.

On 10 May 1832, Mary cancelled a codicil to the will. She stated she had sold the land in Aylesford, Nova Scotia, to Major Pringle Taylor, her nephew. [122]

Stephen 30 July 1766-1767

The twin of Philip, unfortunately, died young in 1767.

Margaret Hughes 1768–9 Sept 1828

Margaret was born on Long Island, New York. In May 1788, in Halifax, Nova Scotia,[123] she married Capt. Onesiphorus Elliott Ovens-Elliott (1761-17 March 1811) of Binfield Park House. He had built the house in 1775 on the 100-acre Binfield Park, Berkshire, England. The couple met when he was serving with the 57th Foot Regiment stationed in Nova Scotia.

---

[121] Caledonian Mercury. 12Apr1813

[122] TNA. PRO B11/1825.

[123] Novascotiagenealogy.com Registration Year: 1788-Book: 1700-Page: 721.

In 1801, Onesiphorus held the role of sheriff of Berkshire. He passed away in March 1811.

In his will, drawn up on 21 June 1810 and proved in London on 30 March 1811, Onesiphorus requested a quiet burial without pomp or ceremony. However, his family laid his body to rest on 21 March in Bath Abbey.[124]

Margaret died on 9 September 1828 at her home in Tidenham Chase. A memorial tablet is in St Mary and St Peter Church on the north wall of the inside of the base of the tower. The church is in the village of Tidenham, Gloucestershire, which is on the Welsh border with Chepstow.

Margaret's situation had changed, and in her will, she left her personal belongings and jewellery to her sisters, Sarah and Charlotte, and her nieces, Elizabeth and Mary Anne Anderson. To her sister Sarah, she left any entitlement she had to land in Aylesford, Nova Scotia.[125]

SACRED TO THE MEMORY
OF MARGARET HUGHES ELLIOTT,
WIDOW OF THE LATE O.E.ELLIOTT ESQ.
OF BINFIELD HOUSE BERKS,
OBIIT 9TH OF SEPTEMBER 1828,
AGED 59 YEARS.

"SHE HATH DONE WHAT SHE COULD."

---

[124] https://www.findagrave.com/memorial/223030664/onesiphorus_elliott-elliott: Bath Abbey Memorials.

[125] TNA PROB11/1759

Sarah Ogden March 1771-18 April 1771

Sarah was born on Long Island and died on 18 April 1771. The family buried her in the Grace Episcopal Churchyard, Jamaica, Queens County, New York.[126]

---

[126] Find A Grave Memorial# 68902344.

Gertrude 1772–3 Oct 1849

Gertrude was Philip and Catharine's first child to be born in their new home in Hanover, Morris, New Jersey. Gertrude, just 17, married Capt. Edward Buller (24 Dec 1764-15 April 1824) of Trenant Park, Duloe, Cornwall, on 15 March 1789 in Halifax, Nova Scotia. The Right Rev. Charles Bishop officiated at the ceremony.

They had 2 children, a boy, John St. Aubyn (1798-25 July 1799), who died aged seventeen months.[127] They buried John on 25 July 1799 at St. Mary's Church at Guys Cliff, Warwickshire.[128]

Their other child was a girl named Anna Maria (3 Nov 1799-26 Feb 1845). The family baptised Anna on 14 November 1799 at Stoke Fleming, Devon.

She married James Drummond Elphinstone (1788-1875) on 25 February 1821 at Duloestone, Clifton, Cornwall.

Edward Buller received promotion to Rear-Admiral in 1808 and was created a baronet later that year. In 1812, he received a promotion to Vice-Admiral. He died at Trenant Park in 1824 and is buried in St Cuby's Graveyard, Duloe, Cornwall.[129]

Edward's will, drawn up on 25 March 1824, left all his estates and money to Gertrude. She and Lieutenant Colonel James Drummond Buller Elphinstone, her son-in-law, were the executors.

Lady Buller, now living at 4 Higher Terrace, Torquay, died on Wednesday, 3 Oct 1849.

---

[127] Naval Chronicle Vol 2, page 448.
[128] "England, Warwickshire, Parish Registers, 1535-1963", FamilySearch (https://www.familysearch.org/ark:/61903/1:1:7JYW-RWW2).
[129] Find a Grave Memorial ID 121595464, citing St Cuby's Graveyard, Duloe, Cornwall Unitary Authority, Cornwall, England;

They buried her at St Andrews Church, Torre, Torquay, Devon, where a plaque is mounted on the inside wall. Gertrude made her will on 15 September and which was proved on 12 November 1849.[130]

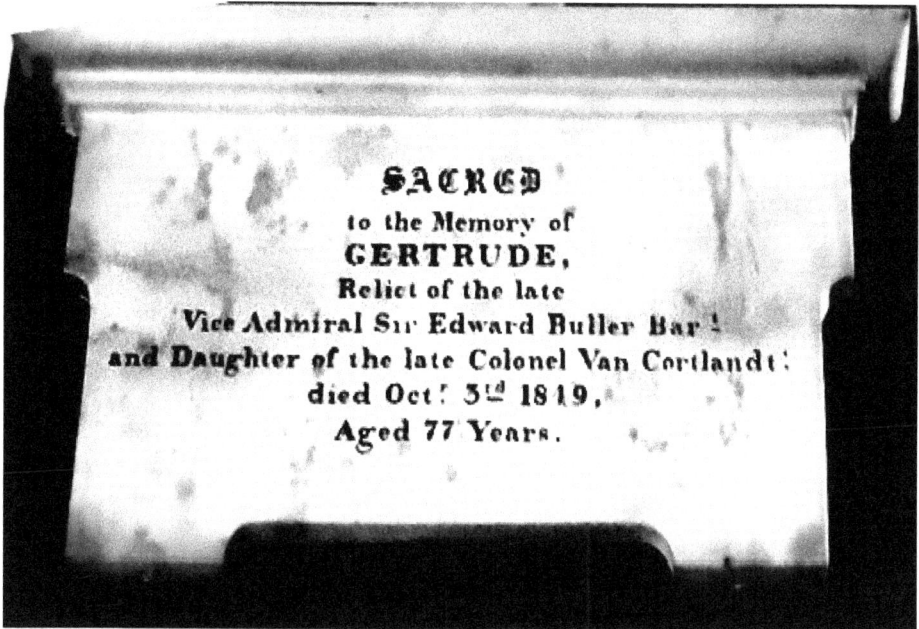

SACRED
to the Memory of
GERTRUDE,
Relict of the late
Vice Admiral Sir Edward Buller Bar.
and Daughter of the late Colonel Van Cortlandt;
died Oct! 3d 1819,
Aged 77 Years.

Sarah Ogden (1774–29 March 1857)

Sarah was born in Hanover, Morris, New Jersey, in 1774. In 1851, Sarah was living at the Grange, Torquay, with her niece, Georgiana Harriet Mulcaster/Harding.

---

[130] TNA PROB11/2102/145/161

Sarah died on 29 March 1857, aged 83, in Old Springs, near Market Drayton, Staffordshire, England.[131] The burial took place on 4 April at St Saviour's Church, Tormoham (Torquay) Parish, Devon, England.[132]

Sarah never married. On 22 May 1854, she made her will and left £100 to her brother, Colonel Henry Clinton. The will was proved on 23 April 1857.[133]

Her niece was the executor of her will and inherited the remainder of her estate.

Richard Willing (Sept 1775-16 March 1778)

Richard was born in Hanover, Morris, New Jersey. After surviving the family journey from Hanover, he died aged 2 years 6 months. They buried him in Grace Episcopal Churchyard, Jamaica, Queens County, New York.[134]

---

[131] Worcester Journal 18Apr1857 and BIRMINGHAM Gazette 06Apr1857

[132] https://www.freebmd.org.uk/cgi/information.pl?cite=pYCavVP53QSUnaKGTVJZCA&scan=1.

[133] TNA PROB11/2250/235/248

[134] Find A Grave Memorial# 68902344.

Jacob Ogden Van Cortlandt (1777-27 Sept 1811)

Jacob was born in New York, and as a young teenager, he joined the Loyal American Regiment as an ensign. Later, after the American War of Independence ended, he joined the British Army and became a senior captain in the 1ˢᵗ Battalion 23ʳᵈ Royal Welch Fusiliers.

Jacob married Anne Warrington (5 May 1774-18 Feb 1870) on 8 October 1805,[135] at Wrexham, Denbighshire, Wales.

Their children were:

George Warrington Van Cortlandt, who was living in 1811, died young.

Emma Van Cortlandt (1810-29 Apr 1879), later Warrington. She died in Wyke House, Wyke Regis, on 29 April 1879.

Jacob died on active service on 27 September 1811 in defence of the village Aldea da Ponte, northeast of Alfayates, in Portugal, during the Napoleonic Wars.

He drew up his will when he was travelling by ship from Liverpool to Spain on 29 October 1810. He left his estate to his wife, Anne. On 17 March 1812, they proved the will in London.[136]

Anne, on 25 December 1815, received a pension from the army and, after applying for assistance, received a further grant of £50 on 30 April 1816.[137]

Between June 1839 and 1859, Anne lived on Jersey in the Channel Islands. In February 1870, Anne died at The Cottage, Wyke Regis, Weymouth, and the probate court in Dorset validated her will on 13 April 1870.

---

[135] TNA WO42. Volume 47. Folio 89.
[136] TNA PROB11/1531/264/351
[137] TNA WO42. Volume 47. Folio 88.

Henry Clinton (1780-1863)

Henry was born in Jamaica, Long Island. Like his father, he joined the British Army. This was in May 1814.

In 1827, he served as a lieutenant of a troop in the 24th Light Dragoons before becoming a captain in the 8th Light Dragoons. He became a lieutenant-colonel in December 1843 of the 31st Foot Regiment[138,] serving in India. In 1837, he received a promotion to major.[139] Henry resigned from the army on 30 December 1843.

There are some reports that indicate Henry married a local Indian woman, possibly an Afghan princess, although they do not record her name. They had a son who also served in India and reached a high rank in the British army. After leaving the army and returning to England, Henry Clinton died at his home in Kensington, London, on 9 May 1863.[140] He was interred in the East Bell Tower Catacombs, Vault D, Brompton Cemetery.

Their children were:

Henry Charles (Feb 1813-15 March 1888).[141] He was born in Meerut, Uttar Pradesh, India and christened on 2 February 1813. After receiving his education in England, he returned to India in 1832. He became a general in the Sikh army.

---

[138] London Gazette December 1843
[139] London Gazette January 1837.
[140] *Find a Grave*, database and images (https://www.findagrave.com/memorial/222108283/henry_clinton-van_cortlandt: accessed March 22, 2025), memorial page for Lt. Col. Henry Clinton Van Cortlandt (1779–9 May 1863),
[141] Brompton Cemetery ID: 221939591, Principal Probate Registry. Calendar of the Grants of Probate and Letters of Administration made in the Probate Registries of the High Court of Justice in England.

When he retired in March 1868; he took up residence at Onslow Crescent, Kensington, living there for twenty years until his death.

Henry Clinton's daughter Elizabeth Margaret (7 Oct 1810-?) /Porter was born in Meerut and baptised on 4 August 1811 in Bengal, India.[142]

Charlotte (1782–18 Dec 1847)

The last child of Philip and Catharine to be born in America.

Charlotte married General Sir John Fraser (24 July 1760-14 Nov 1843) of Campden Hill, Middlesex, England on 15 April 1841.

The ceremony took place in Weymouth[143] and was witnessed by Pringle Taylor, Gertrude Elizabeth Mulcaster and William Henry Waddington.

John died at his home at Campden Hill, Kensington, London, on 14 Nov 1843 and was buried at St Barnabas' Church, Kensington, London.[144]

On 2 July 1844, Charlotte, living in Clifton, Bristol, applied for a widow's pension.[145]

Charlotte, childless, died on 18 December 1847 in Exeter, Devon[146]. They buried her on 27 December in St. Margaret and St. Andrew churchyard in Littleham, Devon. Her will, written on 15 September 1846, was proved in London on 11 February 1848.[147]

---

[142] United Kingdom, British India Office, Births and Baptisms, 1712-1965.
[143] The Spectator 24 April 1841.
[144] Find a Grave Memorial ID 268695081, citing St. Barnabas, Kensington, Royal Borough of Kensington and Chelsea, Greater London, England;
[145] TNA. WO42. Volume 17. Folio F239.
[146] Find a Grave Memorial ID 268694512, citing St. Margaret and St. Andrew Churchyard, Littleham, East Devon District, Devon, England;
[147] TNA PROB11/2069/117/107-8

Jane (1783-1785)

Jane was born in London but unfortunately died young in 1785.

William (May 1785-31 Oct 1785)

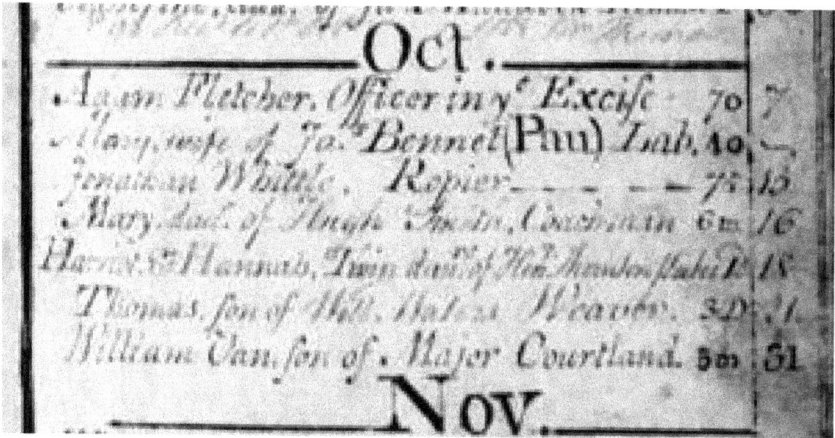

148

William was born in 1785 in Cheshire and died at five months. The family buried him on 31 October in St Oswald Churchyard, Chester, Cheshire. [149]

Arthur Auchmuty (March 1787-11 Nov 1827)

Arthur was born in March 1787 in Funchal, Madeira.

After travelling to Nova Scotia and then England on the 10th of May 1799, Philip and Catharine brought Arthur, aged 12 years and two

---

[148] "England, Cheshire, Parish Registers, 1538-2000", , *FamilySearch* (https://www.familysearch.org/ark:/61903/1:1:FQ6F-JYT :
[149] Burial; citing item 3 p 39, St Oswald, Chester, Cheshire, England, Record Office, Chester; FHL microfilm 2,068,353.

months old, to St Mary's Church, Guys Cliffe in Warwick, England, to be baptised.[150]

A captain in the 45th Regiment, he died in 1827 in Madras, India.[151] He was unmarried.

By an order of the Supreme Court of Judication, they auctioned all his personal goods and possessions in November 1828 at Madras.

Sophia Sawyer 1789–4 Jan 1841

Sophia was born in Halifax, Nova Scotia and married Sir William-Howe Mulcaster (October 1783 -10 March 1837) of Duloe, Cornwall, England, on 13 Oct 1814.[152]

They had 5 children, Gertrude Elizabeth (March 1816-1889) /Beckett, baptised 31 March 1816. Frederick William Edward (1817-1820) baptised on 21 May 1817. William Edward (29 Sep 1820-4 Feb 1887), William Sidney Smith (10 Nov 1825-10 Jan 1910), and Georgiana Harriet (1830-1860) /Harding.

William-Howe died in Dover, Kent, on 12 March 1837 and is buried at St Mary's Church, Bishopsbourne, Kent.[153] Sophia passed away on 4 Jan 1841, four years after her husband. Her burial at All Saints Churchyard took place on the 11th at Wyke Regis, Weymouth.[154]

---

[150] Warwickshire County Record Office; Warwick, England; *Warwickshire Anglican Registers*; Roll: *Engl/2/1249*; Document Reference: *DR 447*.
[151] Death announcements taken from the East India Register.
[152] https://search.findmypast.co.uk/record? id=R_84492 354/2.
[153] Find a Grave Memorial ID 27567142, citing St Mary Churchyard, Bishopsbourne, City of Canterbury, Kent, England;
[154] Dorset Record Office PE/WYR:RE 4/3 https://familysearch.org/pal:/MM9.1.1/2J3B-KTZ.

REFERENCES

Alfred, Jones.E (Edward Alfred) – *The Loyalists of New Jersey; their memorials, petitions, claims etc., from English records.* -1972- Gregg Press, Boston.

Allen, R – *The Loyal Americans* – 1983 – National Museums of Canada.

Burke, John – *History of the Landed Gentry, Vol iv* – Henry Colburn, London.

Burke, John — *History of the Commoners of GB and Ireland Vol iv* – 1868 — Henry Colburn.

Clayton, E.B — *Catalogue of Columbia College* – 1836 — Columbia College, New York.

Clutterbuck, Clare – *Study of Philip van Cortlandt* – Gage family.

Davidson, Stephen – 2010 – Newsletter, Loyalist Trails.

De Lancey, Edward Floyd, — *Origin and History of the Manors in the Province of New York and in the County of Westchester* – 1886 – New York.

De Forest, L. Effingham – *The Van Cortlandt Family*-1930-The Historical Publication Society. NY

Dix, Morgan, — *A History of the Parish of Trinity Church in the City of New York* — 1898 G.P. Putnam's Sons

Dobson, David – *Dutch Colonists in the Americas,1615-1815* – 2008 — Genealogical Publishing Co.

Eaton, Arthur Wentworth Hamilton – *History of Kings County. N.S.* – 1910 — Salem Press Co.

Evans, Thomas Grier – *Records of the Reformed Dutch Church, New York, Baptisms* — 1901

Flick, Alexander Clarence – *Loyalism in New York during the American Revolution* — 1901 – The Columbia University Press, New York.

Gilroy, Marion – *Loyalist and Land settlement in Nova Scotia* – 1937 — Public Archives, N.S.

Gurley, Albert E — *The History & Genealogy of the Gurley Family* – 1897 — Hardford, Conn.

Harland, Marion – *Colonial Homesteads and their Stories* – 1912- G.P.Putnam's Sons.

Haxtun, Annie Arnoux – *Early Settlers of New Amsterdam* Pamphlet IV – 1903 — reprinted from The Mail and Express, New York.

Judd, Jacob — *The Unknown Philip Van Cortlandt: Loyalist* — 1983

Ladd, Horatio Oliver – *The Origins & History of Grace Church, Jamaica, New York.* — 1914

Lee, Francis Bazley -*New Jersey as a Colony and as a State* -Vol 2, 1902 -The Publishing Society of New Jersey.

LeVine, Stephen – *Hailsham Barracks* – 2023 — Loncastle South, Eastbourne.

MacGregor, Gordon – *The Red Book of Scotland* – Vol 4.

Moore, Frank — *Diary of the American Revolution, Vol 1* — Charles Scribner, Grand Street N.Y. -1859 Morris, Ira K. — *Morris's Memorial History of Staten Island NY — Vol 1* – 1898 - Memorial Publishing Co. NY.

Morris, Ira K. – *Morris's Memorial History of Staten Island* – Vol 1- 1898 – Memorial Publishing Company, New York.

Munsell, W. W. — *History of Morris County 1738-1882.*

Munsell, W. W. — *History of Queens County New York* — 1882

New York Historical Society – *Muster rolls of New York Provincial Troops 1755-1764* – 1891

Onderdonk, Henry jnr – *The Revolutionary Incidents of Queens County* – 1864 — Leavitt, Trow & Co. Broadway, New York.

Pelletreau, William S – *Early Wills of Westchester NY from 1664-1784* – 1898 – New York — Francis P Harper.

Pine, John B — 1917 — *King's College & the Early days of Columbia College* — NY State Historical Society.

Public Archives of Nova Scotia – Loyalists and Land Settlement in N.S. – pages 64/5

Raymond, W.O. – *Roll of Officers AD 1775-1783 of the British American or Loyalist Corp.*

Rink, Oliver A. -*Holland on the Hudson: An Economic and Social History of Dutch New York,* Ithaca, NY: Cornell, 1986;

Roebling, Emily Warren – *Journal of the Rev Silas Constant* — 1903– Lippincott Co. Philadelphia.

Rogers, Rev Charles — *Memorials of the Scottish House of Gourlay* — Private Print Edinburgh.

Ryan, Dennis P. – *New Jersey's Loyalist* – 1975 — New Jersey Historical Commission

Siebert, Wilbur. H – *The Flight of American Loyalists to the British Isles* – 1911 -The F. J. Herr Printing Co.

Slye, Matthias — *Diary of Matthias Slye, Farmer* — Hailsham — 2nd Edition.

Sprague, William. B – *Annals of the American Pulpit* – Vol 5 – 1859 - Robert Carter & Bros, N.Y.

Stryker, William E –1887 — *The New Jersey Volunteers (Loyalists) In the Revolutionary War.* — Naar, Day 7 Naar. Trenton. N.J.

Sullivan, Dr. James – *The History of NYS* — Book12, Chapter16, Part6

Tucker, Gideon J – *Marriage Licenses issued prior to 1784 – 1860 –* Weed, Parsons & Co

The Dutch Settlers Society of Albany – Vol. V. Yearbook 1929-1930

The New York Gazette – various.

The New York Genealogical and Biographical Record — Vol: 1,5,18. — 1874 – Society N.Y.

The New York Genealogical & Biographical Society – 2006 – King's (now Columbia) College.

Van Tyne, Claude Halstead – *The Loyalists in the American Revolution* – 1902 – The Macmillan Company. New York.

Valentine, David Thomas – *History of the city of New York* – G. P. Putham & Company. 1853

Vernon-Jackson, H. O. H., *"A Loyalist's Wife: Letters of Mrs. Philip Van Cortlandt December 1776 to February 1777"*, History Today Magazine, Volume XIV, no. 8, Pages 574-580.

Wardell, Pat — *Early Bergen County Families* — The Genealogical Society of Bergen Co. N.J.

Wendell, John L – *Reports of cases in the Supreme Court for the correction of errors of the State of New York* – Vol XX 1846

Wheeler, William Ogden. (2013). pp. 71, 191,265-6. *The Ogden Family in America, Elizabethtown Branch, and Their English Ancestry.* London: Forgotten Books. (Original work published 1907).

Wilkins, Isaac – *My Services & Losses in aid of the King's Cause during the American Revolution* – 1890 – Brooklyn, N.Y. Historical Printing Club.

Manchester Mercury 19 June 1787.

Van Cortlandt Papers, Vol. 1, Mary Lucy Cortlandt and Anderson Mulcaster, National Army Museum Library, Chelsea

Websites:

http://binfield.co.uk/information/binfield-history/
http://www.newnetherlandinstitute.org/history-and-heritage/dutch_americans/oloff-van-cortlandt/
http://rnfldr.ca The Royal Newfoundland Regiment.
https://royalprovincial.com
https://storymaps.arcgis.com/stories/75b86f04812e4df996c7d75684bdc5f2

****

ABOUT THE AUTHOR

Stephen leVine was born in London and educated in Hove, Sussex, and London. After many years of travelling worldwide, working for a holiday tour company, he returned to England. He opened his own business, moved in 1985 to Hailsham, Sussex and became a resident of Eastbourne in 1987. With a keen interest in history, this is his seventh book.

Other titles from the author:

Lords to Bureaucrats
A History of Sussex Town Halls and their local benefactors.
ISBN:-9780993544101

Hailsham Barracks
A Napoleonic Defence 1803 – 1815
ISBN:- 9798223436331

Unsung Heroes,
Eastbourne's Fire Service 1824-1974
ISBN:- 9780993544132

The Sitakund Disaster.
A story of fire and explosions in the English Channel in 1968.
ISBN:- 9780993544149

Six ships, one name.
The travels and adventures of very different vessels
ISBN:- 9780993544163

www.ingramcontent.com/pod-product-compliance
Lightning Source LLC
Chambersburg PA
CBHW062215080426
42734CB00010B/1895